# HOME
# REPAIRS AND
# IMPROVEMENTS

## Edited by R. H. Allen

**GUILD PUBLISHING**
LONDON

Original material © Marshall Cavendish Limited 1986/87
This edition © Marshall Cavendish Limited 1989

This edition published 1989
by Guild Publishing
by arrangement with
Marshall Cavendish Limited,
58 Old Compton Street, London W1V 5PA
CN 3281

Printed in Portugal

# CONTENTS

# INTRODUCTION

Home improvement has two main results: to improve the quality of life in your home; and to increase the value of the property. Carrying out these improvements yourself has the additional result of giving you the satisfaction of enjoying your own workmanship for years to come. This book sets out to give you full instructions for completing a variety of projects with confidence.

The book is arranged in sections, each containing a selection of 'new' projects and maintenance tasks. Take a kitchen, for example—the first room in many a house to receive attention. In the Home Plumber section you will find instructions for curing a dripping tap and plumbing in a washing machine. Would the room be more convenient if the door opened the other way? The Home Carpenter section tells you how to rehang a door and make any necessary repairs to it. Condensation and cooking smells can be a problem—you will find instructions for installing an extractor fan in Home Builder. And what use would an extractor fan be without electricity? Home Electrician solves that problem and gives details of the wiring circuits for a selection of kitchen appliances. There is also a comprehensive index for locating information that may not necessarily have a full article devoted to it.

Before attempting any of the projects, it is a good idea to read through the instructions from start to finish to give yourself a clear idea of what is involved. If, after doing so, you are unsure of your capabilities, try to enlist the help of a friend with more experience of such things— you can learn so much in this way and boost your confidence to tackle a similar job yourself the next time. This is especially important in the case of electricity where mistakes can have serious consequences—if in doubt, contact a qualified electrician!

If you are a novice at DIY, tackle the simple jobs first before attempting the more ambitious ones and enjoy your achievements. If you are an old hand, you will find this book an invaluable source of reference. Whatever the level of your skill, you will find here ways to improve and maintain the value of any home. Applying a little time and money now can bring great benefits in the years to come.

G. *A shower enclosure can be incorporated in an under-stairs conversion where other simple washing facilities may also be provided for use by occasional guests. Lack of privacy may pose a problem, however*

# Install an electric shower

An instant electric shower is an attractive proposition if use cannot be made of conventional hot and cold water supplies. In most instances, connection of the heater is direct to the mains water supply—so a shower of this type is especially useful if a hot water cylinder is not incorporated within the system. Pressure and flow variations within the system may have a marked effect on temperature stability, however. The heater needs direct and permanent connection to the electricity supply through a double-pole linked switch. The appliance must be earthed, and protected by a 30amp fuse. For additional safety, site the heater well away from the direct spray at the shower, and locate the switch outside the bathroom or shower enclosure.

You can interrupt the rising main at any convenient point. Remember to keep the pipe run as short and as straight as possible. This Deltaflow unit requires a cold water supply which has a minimum static pressure of one bar (equivalent to a water head of about eight metres) which should be available from most mains supplies. In most houses, though, you cannot use a cistern-fed supply because the head will not be great enough.

In Australia and New Zealand you must have electric and plumbing work done by licenced tradesmen. Heater suppliers usually provide a complete installation service.

the fitting by pushing the triple socket down into its final position.

Insert the spigot bend into the boss branch, attach brackets to the outside connecting length of the discharge pipe and fit this into the spigot bend. Twist the boss branch until the supporting brackets on the discharge pipe make contact with the wall.

The discharge pipe from the inside of the house should by now meet the discharge pipe attached to the stack, and the two can be marked for cutting so that you can fit a 90° bend where the inner pipe leaves the wall. Remove both pipes and cut these to final length.

Replace all pipes, the longer (outside) one with its fixing brackets in place. The shorter (inner) length is fixed first to the trap and then to the bend. Screw the trap to the waste outlet of the shower base. It is essential that all pipes and fittings are perfectly aligned and that no force is used to keep them in place. Make minor adjustments if necessary.

Mark and fix supporting brackets, normally required only for the outside length. Make alignment marks at each of the fittings.

Dismantle pipework and fittings that require solvent welded joints, prepare the joints and reassemble as before.

If the discharge pipe is to be led to an outside hopper, cut the protruding pipe close to the wall and fit a 90° bend. Attach whatever length of pipe is necessary to complete the run to a convenient point above the hopper, and provide support brackets.

Make good the hole through the wall using a proprietary filler paste. There are now aerosol foam sprays on the market which are waterproof, allow for expansion or contraction, and are easier to work with than the more traditional compounds.

Test the pipework, first for stability (proper support and correct joining) and then for watertightness, using a pail of water until connection is made with the supply system.

Connection of the hot and cold water supply pipes to the shower controller (or regulator) is made in the course of assembling the shower enclosure, and the procedures should follow exactly those stipulated by the manufacturer. The valve and spray piping are attached to a mounting panel attached to the wall or set into the wall along with piping. With self-contained shower enclosures, the mounting panel is attached to the rear of the cubicle with a waterproof gasket arrangement.

## Completing the enclosure

Once the shower base installation is complete, you can attend to the completion of the shower enclosure. This is a relatively simple job if you are using a prefabricated kit, which often requires little more than a few minutes with a screwdriver. Built-in enclosures requiring woodwork, tiling and other jobs (not forgetting suitable sealing at the joints) take much longer to make but can be matched completely to the design of the room.

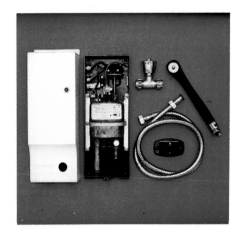

**1** *An instant electric shower heater usually comes as a kit of parts. Installation involves plumbing and electrical skills*

**2** *Remove the cover and mark the position of the fixing holes, and drill for fixings as required. Knock through for connecting wires*

**3** *Cable entry to heater is best made through the rear. Ensure this is correctly wired, tightening the cable clamp securely afterwards*

**4** *The double-pole linked switch is located safely on the other side of the wall and connected to the heater via the wall aperture*

**5** *Pipe connections near to the heater can be tailor-made to fit. Use capillary fittings up to the point the heater fitting is used*

**6** *Interrupt the cold water supply wherever is most convenient, using a 'T' connector. In a loft, lag the pipe well*

**7** *Mark the shower rail position and screw the rail firmly into position, with the top of the rail no higher than the heater*

**8** *Connect the flexible hose to the water outlet of the heater, turn on the water mains and the flow tap and then check pipework for leaks*

**9** *Repeat the procedure with the heater on. Where water pressure is too high, the restrictor may need adjusting to reduce the maximum flow*

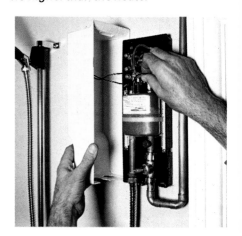

**10** *When tests have been completed to your satisfaction, finally replace the cover and connect the two neon spade leads*

# PLUMBING IN A WASHING MACHINE

● **Choosing the best site** ● **Breaking into the existing water supply** ● **Connecting the hot and cold supplies** ● **Installing the branch discharge pipe** ● **Connection to a back inlet gulley** ● **Connection to a soil stack**

*Left: Though the way in which the hot and cold water supplies are connected varies from machine to machine, hoses are often used at the machine end. This gives you more flexibility in your choice of site and permits easy removal for cleaning*

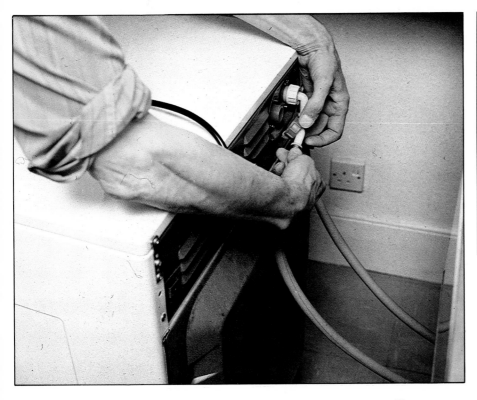

## Check first!

In the UK, plumbing work is strictly controlled by local water authority by-laws. You must inform your water authority of your plans at least seven days before work starts. As well as giving practical advice, they will warn you against any possible infringement of their regulations. Work on the drainage system may need building regulations consent.

In Australia/NZ, only a licensed plumber is authorised to extend or repair any household plumbing.

Though an automatic washing machine is a boon to any household, many people are discouraged from buying one because it has to be plumbed in—both to the water supply and the drains. But providing you choose the site carefully and set about the work in a logical order, the job is not half as hard as it seems.

The work can be divided into four stages: positioning the machine; connecting up the cold water supply (probably hot, too, though many machines are cold-fill only); installing a branch discharge pipe to the drains; making the electrical connections. The last step involves plugging into a socket outlet or fitting a fused connection unit.

### Choosing a site

Your first decision here is in which room to site the machine. In the UK, the choice is normally between the kitchen and bathroom, both of which have hot and cold water supplies and drainage outlets. In Australia, the

usual site is a basement utility room.

You have next to consider the type of machine, the space that will be needed around it, the existing layout of the room and the design and materials used in your plumbing system.

Of these, the plumbing system must inevitably take priority. It is no use choosing the ideal space-saving site only to find that you cannot then plumb in the machine without demolishing the house.

**Drainage:** In the UK, for a washing machine in a ground floor kitchen, the most suitable outlet for the discharge pipe is a back inlet gully, separated from the main discharge stack and connected to the main drain by a branch underground. This is often easier to break into than the main stack and, as it is usually there to serve the kitchen sink discharge pipe, it is likely to be in the most convenient position already.

In older houses, the sink waste sometimes discharges over an open,

trapped gully leading to the drains. You will probably be allowed to run the washing machine discharge pipe to here also, provided that the end of the pipe is below the grid.

If the pipe has to connect to the main stack, the latter will need a branch fitting. Though this is relatively easy to fit to a plastics stack, on the older, cast-iron or galvanized steel types the job is best left to an expert. Indeed, it is probably better to take the opportunity of replacing the stack with a new one. A connection to an existing hopper head may not be allowed; check with your local council's building department.

**Water supply:** Breaking into the hot and cold water supply generally presents less of a problem, as the final connections to the machine are usually made with flexible hose. Nevertheless, the supply must be near enough to the site to allow you to keep pipe runs as short—and as simple—as possible.

In the UK, a cold-only supply might come direct from the rising main (usually the easiest arrangement if the machine is in a kitchen), though some water authorities do not allow this.

A hot and cold fill machine is best supplied via the cold water storage cistern or tank. In this case, as with some showers, low water pressure is sometimes a problem on upper floors or in flats and bungalows. Manufacturers

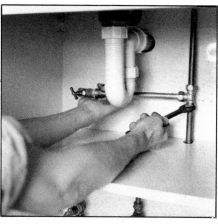

**1** *Having isolated and drained down the pipes, sever them with a fine toothed hacksaw. Make the cuts as cleanly as possible*

**2** *With careful planning, you can keep the run simple and the number of joints to a minimum. Use compression or capillary joints*

**3** *With some types of valve, the flexible hose ends may simply screw on, as here. With other types different fixings will be needed*

generally specify a minimum 'head' of water—that is, the distance from the base of the storage tank to the point where the supply enters the back of the washing machine—and you should bear this in mind when choosing a site for your machine. If you cannot meet the minimum head requirement, consult both the manufacturer and your local water authority.

In Australia, an automatic washing

machine is almost always connected direct to mains pressure supply.

The pipe run must be arranged so that the branches do not cross one another, with the stop valves easily accessible. When you are planning the run, consider the best place to fit tee pieces to the supply pipes; it may be better to have a slightly longer run in order to avoid disturbing existing fixtures and fittings.

## Breaking into the supply

Having chosen your supply pipes, turn off the stop valves that are nearest to them and drain off the pipes by opening the taps at the end of each pipe run. With cistern-fed supplies, if there

**A. Below:** *A typical completed installation. Note that in some areas, taking the cold supply direct from the rising main is not allowed*

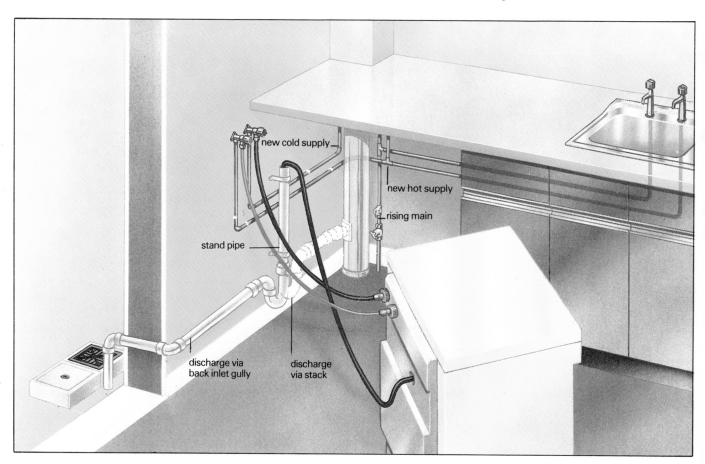

new cold supply

new hot supply

rising main

stand pipe

discharge via
back inlet gully

discharge
via stack

**3** Cut copper tubing with a pipe cutter or a hacksaw fitted with a fine toothed blade and clean up the burr with a fine file

**4** Bend copper tubing with a pipe bender, or use a spring or rubber 'bendable core' (to stop kinks) and manipulate the tube over your knee

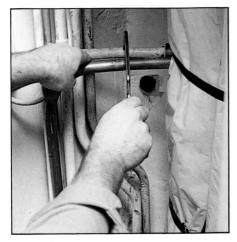

**5** Locate the primary circuit flow pipe (on the side of the hot water cylinder) and cut through it along a convenient straight run

water towel rail is well worth considering. The plain tubular sort offer plenty of towel hanging space and generally produce enough heat to keep the average size bathroom at a constantly comfortable temperature. They can be plumbed in to the house hot water system—rather than the radiator circuit—so that they remain hot even when the heating is switched off—in the summer, say. And, as most bathrooms have a hot water cylinder close at hand, this makes installation straightforward.

Some hot water rails include a radiator panel to provide extra heating facilities, but these can be fitted only to indirect type heating systems where there is no risk of them becoming clogged with scale. Tubular rails, on the other hand, can be installed in any

hot water system—direct or indirect—which incorporates a storage tank/boiler/hot water cylinder arrangement.

### Identifying your water system

Before you plumb-in a hot water towel rail, it is obviously important to know what type of hot water system you have and to identify the pipes.

In the older, direct system, water heated by the boiler rises by thermal convection to the hot water cylinder. Here, it continues to rise until it passes out of the top (crown) to the hot taps, via the hot water supply pipe. Fresh water is fed to the system from the cold storage tank and enters via the base of the cylinder. From here, it sinks to the boiler under force of gravity.

If no water is drawn off the hot taps, the water in the system continues to circulate between the cylinder and the boiler. When hot water is used, fresh water is taken in and heated to the desired temperature.

Although simple, the main drawback of the direct system is scale. This is released every time fresh water is heated above about 60°C and clogs cylinder and boiler pipework alike. In the indirect system—most often found with central heating—the problem of scale is avoided by having two separate circuits. The first—known as the primary circuit—runs continuously between the boiler and cylinder. The water in it is always hot, but because it is never drawn off it is introduced fresh only once. Consequently, it releases its scale the first time it is heated and from then onwards it is relatively scale-free.

The hot water cylinder in an indirect system contains a loop—the

heat exchanger—through which the hot primary circuit water passes. As it does so, it transfers its heat to fresh water fed to the base of the cylinder from the cold storage tank. This fresh water then becomes hot—but not hot enough to release scale—and rises out of the crown of the cylinder to feed the hot taps in the normal way. The cold feed, the outer part of the cylinder and the pipework supplying the hot taps comprise what is known as the secondary circuit.

Both direct and indirect systems contain vent pipes to guard against the build-up of excessive pressure. The direct system has a single vent pipe, rising from the crown of the cylinder, or the hot tap supply pipe, to above the cold storage tank. The indirect system has this pipe too, plus another rising from the primary circuit flow pipe to above the expansion tank.

The function of the expansion tank in an indirect system is to top up the water in the primary circuit, should some be lost by leakage or evaporation, and to allow for the slight expansion of the water as it is heated. The flow in the primary circuit may be by gravity—as in the direct system—or included in the radiator circuit and under pump pressure. In the latter case, a motorized valve distributes water from the boiler between the cylinder heat exchanger and the radiators as and where it is required.

### Making the connection

Hot water towel rails work on the same principle as radiators, with two connection points for flow and return pipes. In both direct and indirect systems, pipes can run from these to intercept the hot water flow pipe between the boiler and the hot water cylinder. This pipe is cut, and T-shaped connectors inserted to make the final connections (fig. 6).

Obviously, it is absolutely essential to know which pipes are which before you connect to them. This may call for a bit of detective work—particularly in the case of an indirect system—before you go any further. But in any case you should aim to make the connections somewhere around the hot water cylinder. Here, the pipes are easier to identify.

**Direct systems:** Most direct cylinders have four pipes running from them (fig. B). Of the two near the crown, the lower is the flow pipe from the boiler which supplies the cylinder with hot water. The other is the hot water supply pipe, which supplies the hot taps and generally also holds the

# Making the connection

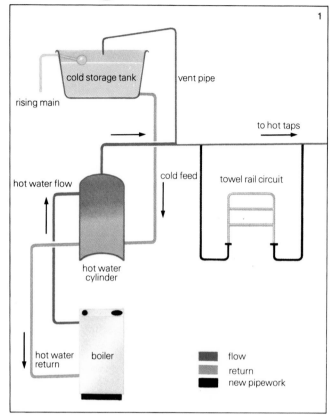

1

- cold storage tank
- vent pipe
- rising main
- to hot taps
- hot water flow
- cold feed
- towel rail circuit
- hot water cylinder
- hot water return
- boiler

flow
return
new pipework

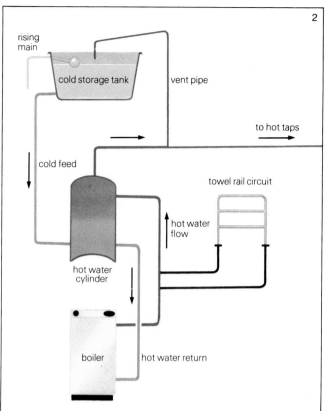

2

- rising main
- cold storage tank
- vent pipe
- cold feed
- to hot taps
- towel rail circuit
- hot water flow
- hot water cylinder
- boiler
- hot water return

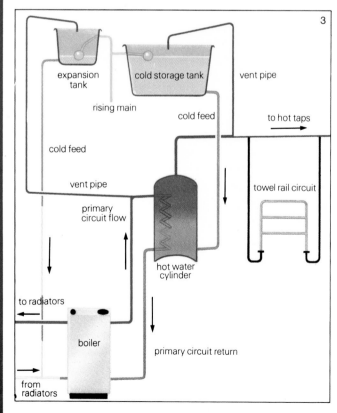

3

- expansion tank
- cold storage tank
- vent pipe
- rising main
- cold feed
- to hot taps
- cold feed
- vent pipe
- primary circuit flow
- towel rail circuit
- hot water cylinder
- to radiators
- boiler
- primary circuit return
- from radiators

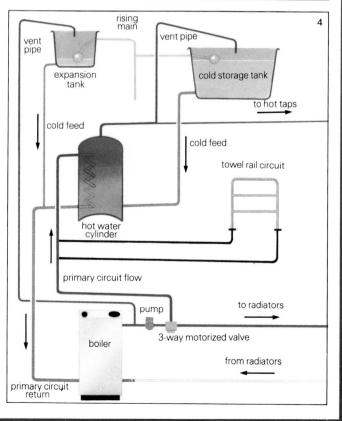

4

- rising main
- vent pipe
- vent pipe
- expansion tank
- cold storage tank
- cold feed
- to hot taps
- cold feed
- towel rail circuit
- hot water cylinder
- primary circuit flow
- pump
- to radiators
- boiler
- 3-way motorized valve
- from radiators
- primary circuit return

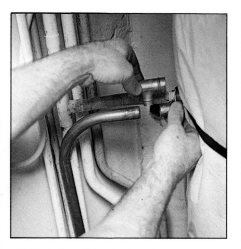

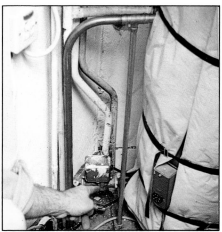

6 *To take off the hot water you must insert T-connectors into the flow pipe. You can use either compression or capillary fittings*

7 *Fix the T-connectors in place, then run copper tubing from the site of the heated towel rail back to the cylinder and join it up*

8 *In the case of a solid floor, bury the piping in a channel 100mm deep. The pipe must be protected with a suitable insulating cover*

vent pipe. In some cases, the vent rises directly from the cylinder (in which case there will be a total of five pipe connections).

Of the two near the base, one is the cold feed from the cold storage tank and the other is the return taking back cooled water to the boiler.

**Indirect system:** Indirect cylinders have the same hot supply vent pipe at the crown and cold feed at the base as direct ones. But the primary flow and return pipes to and from the boiler generally run into the side of the cylinder and stand out from the rest of the pipework. An additional complication is the primary circuit vent pipe. This may pass near the water cylinder, or it may be connected to the flow pipe.

About the only safe way to identify

**Left:** *A direct central heating system* **(1)** *has a single circuit in which the heated water is shared by the radiators and hot taps. Installing the towel rail circuit in the feed to the hot taps means that it works only when hot water is being taken (for example, at bathtime). Installing the towel rail in the hot water feed to the storage cylinder* **(2)** *gives it a constant supply of hot water and is more satisfactory. An indirect central heating system* **(3)** *has two circuits in which the water heated for the radiators is separate from the hot water circuit. The towel rail may be inserted in the hot water circuit (as in* **(1)**), *or* **(4)** *in the primary flow circuit which allows it to be controlled independently of both the radiators and the hot water taps for greater flexibility*

9 *Mark the position of the towel rail fixing holes on the wall and floor, then drill them with a masonry bit and insert wall plugs*

10 *Secure the towel rail in place with the screws provided, but do not tighten the screws until each one has been started*

the pipes is to trace each one in turn and then label it clearly somewhere near the connection point. Once you have the found the flow and return to the boiler, search for a suitable interception point on the flow pipe. This should preferably be on a straight, horizontal run. Make sure, too, that there will be room to work and that the pipe route to the rail will not be too tortuous.

**Installation**

Once you have decided on a site for the rail and identified the connection points, you are ready to begin installation. On all types of hot water system, the first job is to turn off the boiler and allow both pipes and cylinder to cool down. What you do next depends on the type of system.

**Direct system:** In this case it is preferable to turn off the cold water supply at the cold storage tank—rather than at the rising main—so that you will still have use of the kitchen cold tap. If there is no stop valve, tie up the ball valve in the closed position (fig. 1).

Drain the cold tank by opening all taps fed from it, then drain down the hot water system. Attach a hose to the drain cock, which should be located adjacent to the boiler in the return pipe, and having placed the other end of the hose at a suitable drainage point, open the cock.

With the cylinder empty, the hot water flow pipes can be cut using a fine toothed hacksaw and the T-shaped fittings connected. Since only one radiator/rail is to be served, the pipe

11 Smear jointing compound on the threads of the towel rail connecting sockets before you screw on the wheel and lockshield valves

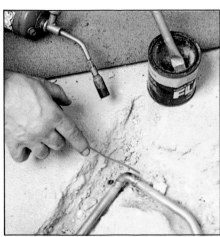

12 Route the copper piping into place then secure all the joints to complete the circuit. Try to use capillary fittings where you can

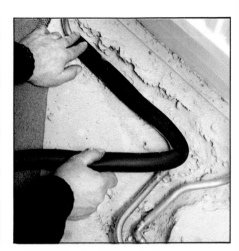

13 When all the connections have been made, you must clad the piping for protection where it passes through walls or floors

14 Turn on the water supply and allow the system to fill up. Check for any leaks, then make good with a cement/sharp sand mortar mix

15 Finally you must bleed each radiator in the system in order to expel any air which may have found its way into it

runs from the teeing points to the site of the unit can usually be of 15mm copper tube.

Assuming that the bathroom is on the first floor, and the floor itself is a conventional joist and board structure, the pipes should run by the shortest possible route under the floorboards. If they must run across joists, notch them into the tops of the joists, resting them on small pads of pipe insulation. Where changes of direction are necessary, use elbow compression fittings or bend the pipe with a bending spring.

If running the pipes under the floor is not feasible, soldered capillary fittings are less obtrusive—and cheaper—than the compression type. Where changes of direction are necessary in surface piping, bend the pipe in preference to using bulky ready-made fittings for a neater finish.

If the bathroom is on a solid ground floor, it may be possible to run the pipes in the ceiling void, then down to connect to the towel rail. The connections to the rail are made with normal radiator valve fittings, a wheel valve with a turnable head on the flow (hot supply) side, and a lockshield valve with a screw-fixed cap on the return side. These compression-joint to the pipes, which must be cut to length once the rail is in place.

Unlike radiators, which are usually hung on brackets fixed to the wall, towel rails—including those incorporating radiator panels—are fixed to the floor by screws passing through their flanged feet. Some also have flanges at the top so that you can fix

them to the wall for added stability.

With the unit fixed and the connections made, check that all taps and drain cocks are closed, open the air vent—normally located under the top rail of a towel rail—and restore the water supply. As the system fills, watch for water appearing at the rail vent. When it does so, close the vent, restart the boiler and run it for about half an hour. Then re-open the vent to release any trapped air in the towel rail itself, with a small pot under the valve to catch any water.

Indirect systems: Here, there is no need to shut off the water at the main cold storage tank or drain the hot water cylinder. Instead, cut off the supply to the expansion tank, attach a hose to the central heating system drain cock—which should be located on the boiler return pipe at its lowest point—and open the cock.

The water in the system should contain rust-inhibiting chemicals, and you may feel it worth collecting the drained water in containers to be put back into the system when you refill it rather than buy a new supply.

Having drained the system completely, proceed as for a direct hot water system. When the installation is complete, refill the system by restoring the cold supply at the expansion tank. After filling, turn all your radiator valves to the fully open position and bleed the radiators in turn to remove airlocks. When you are opening lockshield valves, count how many turns it takes, and afterwards close them by the same number. You may find that the system needs further bleeding after several days, but this is perfectly normal.

a solid fuel boiler, rake the fire into the ashpan and remove it.

If the house feels abnormally hot, check the time clock and, if there is one, the room thermostat. These may be failing to turn the pump off when they should or have had their settings accidentally advanced. Start by turning the time clock down to the present setting. If the radiators do not cool down at the time they are supposed to, the mechanism of the clock has probably jammed and will have to be replaced with a new one.

To check a room thermostat, turn it down to its lowest setting and then back up again. A click should be heard as the switch inside turns the pump on. If there is no click, the unit will have to be replaced.

If the whole system is overheating seriously, the radiator pipes may make prolonged knocking or hissing noises and there will be excessive temperature in the boiler delivery pipe. One possible reason for this is failure of the circulation pump.

To find out whether the pump is working, hold one end of a screwdriver against the casing with the other end to your ear and listen for the hum of the rotor inside (fig. 2): if there is no noise, this is probably stuck. On pumps with a screw-on glass inspection cover, the rotor can be freed quite easily. Turn the pump off, unscrew the cover and insert a screwdriver into one of the slots in the rotor. If the rotor does not spin freely, it should be possible to free it by levering gently with the screwdriver (fig. 4).

On pumps which have all metal casings, the water supply must be cut off before opening the cover. In most cases, there are stop valves on each side for this purpose but where no such valves are fitted, the system will have to be drained before carrying out any work on the pump.

If the pump is heard to be working but water is evidently not circulating, there is probably an air lock. At the top of the pump you will find a vent valve—operated either by a key or a screwdriver—from which the pump can be bled (fig. 5).

To do this, turn the pump off and leave it for a few hours to allow the water in the system to settle. Then open the valve to bleed the air off. A hiss of air will be followed by a trickle of water: when the trickle becomes constant, close the valve.

If the fault is not in the pump, the boiler thermostat may have failed. The thermostat, a small box with a dial on the top, is located behind the boiler casing. Remove the casing and check

that the electrical connections on the thermostat are sound. Check also that the sender bulb on the end of the copper capillary from the thermostat to the boiler has not fallen out of its socket (fig. 7). If so reposition it and replace the securing clip.

Note the setting on the boiler thermostat dial and turn it down low. After a few minutes turn it back towards its maximum setting and listen for a click. If there is no click, it may mean that the thermostat has jammed and you should call in a qualified engineer to check it.

If the boiler thermostat appears to be working, check to see whether the boiler flue outlet outside has become blocked in some way. Depending on the nature of the blockage, expert help may be needed in order to clear it.

If the flue is free of any obstruction, the next thing to check is the expansion tank. The ball valve supplying it may have become jammed or seized, in which case there may not be enough water in the system to absorb the heating action of the boiler. If the level in the tank is more than 150mm from the valve outlet, free the valve and introduce more water into the system. Where the valve is completely seized, replace it with a new ballcock, arm and piston unit.

## Central heating too cool

If all the radiators are cool and the boiler is working correctly, the fault probably lies with one of the thermostats, the time clock or circulation pump. Carry out checks outlined above under 'Overheating', paying special attention to the position of a room thermostat if fitted. This reacts to the temperature around it, and a nearby heat source can cause it to give a false reading even though the mechanism may be perfectly sound.

To work efficiently, the thermostat should be mounted on an internal wall at least 1.5m above the floor and away from draughts, radiators and direct sunlight. It should not be placed in rooms which are in constant use—such as lounges—because people generate extra heat, nor in kitchens, because of the heat from cooking and appliances. However, it should be accessible so that changes in setting can be made conveniently.

## Draining the system

Before doing any major repairs or modifications to your central heating, you will have to drain, or partially drain the system. Start by turning the boiler off and leaving the system for a few hours to cool down. Turn off the

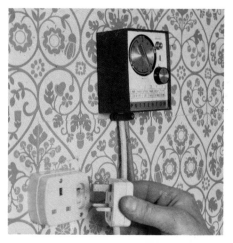

**9** Before draining a central heating system, turn off the electricity supply to the time clock and also to the immersion heater, if fitted

**10** To shut off the water supply to the boiler, close the stop valve tap on the pipe which leads into the expansion tank

electricity supply to the time clock and the immersion heater—if the system includes one (fig. 9).

Shut off the water supply to the boiler by closing the stop valve on the pipe into the expansion tank (fig. 10). If no stop valve is fitted, lash the ball valve in the expansion tank to a piece of wood laid across the tank.

When the system has cooled, return to the boiler and identify the main drain cock. This is usually at the front end of the boiler near the pump where it is always built into the lowest pipe. Alternatively, it may be found on a ground floor radiator. Attach one end of a garden hose to the nozzle and run the other to an outside drain. Open the drain cock by turning the nut beneath with a spanner or adjustable wrench and allow as much water as you require to drain away (fig. 12).

**11** When the system has cooled down, attach one end of a garden hose to the nozzle of the main drain cock on the boiler

**12** Run the other end of the hose to an outside drain, then open the drain cock by turning the nut beneath with an adjustable wrench

### Refilling the system
Before refilling, close the main drain cock securely. Open the valve on the pipe leading to the expansion tank, or untie the ball valve, to admit fresh water into the system. Regulate the position of the valve so that the tank fills slowly—keeping the risk of air locks to a minimum. Also check the drain cock for leaks.

### Noise
Noise is another common problem with wet central heating systems. Creaking under the floorboards and around radiators is caused by pipes—which expand and contract according to the temperature of the water—rubbing against the floor joists on which they rest. Creaking can also occur where a pipe rises through the floorboards to feed a radiator.

The creaking can often be reduced by turning the boiler thermostat down so that the radiators remain switched on for longer periods instead of constantly heating up and cooling down.

If the noise persists, take up the floorboards around the suspect area. Eventually you will find a point where one or two pipes cross a joist and are notched into the woodwork. If the notch is so small that it causes the pipes to rub against each other, enlarge it to give a better clearance. Make sure, though, that the notch does not exceed one sixth of the depth of the joist or it will seriously weaken the timber. Use a piece of rubber pipe lagging, felt or carpet, trimmed to the approximate size of the notch, to cushion the pipes (fig. 13).

Where a pipe rises through a gap in a floorboard, either enlarge the gap by filing it away or pack the space around the pipe with padding (fig. 14). Metal pipe brackets—another common source of noise—can be bent back slightly, and stuffed with felt to prevent them making direct contact with the pipes (fig. 15).

Creaking behind radiators is usually caused by the hooks on the back of the panels rubbing against their corresponding wall brackets. For serious cases, on smaller radiators, special nylon brackets can be fitted in place of the normal pressed steel type. A simpler solution is to place pieces of felt or butyl (rubber) between each hook and bracket. This can be done, with the help of an assistant, by gently lifting the radiator away from its brackets, slipping the pieces of felt into the hooks and then replacing it.

### Immersion heaters
In many systems, hot water for sinks and baths is heated by a thermostatically controlled immersion heater in addition to the boiler-fed heat exchanger in the cylinder. The thermostat is pre-set to turn the heating element off when the water reaches the selected temperature. If the water is unbearably hot, the thermostat may simply need adjusting.

The thermostat control is found at the top or on the side of the hot water cylinder (fig. 16). To adjust it, turn off the electricity supply to the heater then unscrew the element cover where you will find a small dial marked centigrade, fahrenheit, or both. By hand, or with a screwdriver, turn the regulator screw to the desired temperature—normally 60°C (140°F) in hard water areas or 80°C (180°F) in those with especially soft water.

If the water heats up slowly, or the

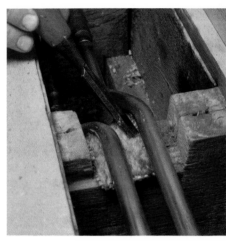

**13** Pipes often creak where they run through a notch in a floor joist. Cushion the pipes with felt or carpet to stop the noise

**14** A pipe may rub against wood where it rises through the floor. Pack the gap round the pipe with pieces of suitable padding

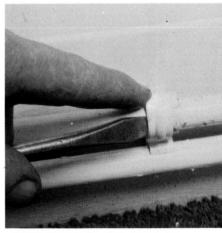

**15** Metal pipe brackets are another common source of noise. Bend them back slightly and stuff pieces of felt into the gaps

**7** *Having located the lock body in position and made any necessary adjustments to the depth of the rebate, screw on the cover plate*

**8** *The only work left on the door itself is to fix the keyhole covers. Make sure the one with the draught cover goes on the inside*

**9** *With the lock closed and held against the door frame, you can mark the depth of the striking plate rebate and bolt box*

**10** *Cut out the hole for the bolt box and striking plate in the frame. Before securing the plate, make sure that the door will close properly*

**11** *Both sides of the finished lock. The design is such that the woodwork around the door will fail before the lock itself*

**12** *Provide additional protection for your front door by installing a pair of hinge bolts. These fit into recesses in the frame*

**13** *A door security chain or bar allows you to open the front door slightly to unknown callers. Fixings must be strong*

## Fitting the striking plate

All that now remains is to fit the striking plate and bolt box onto the door frame.

To mark the position of the rebate, turn the key in the mortise lock so that the bolt protrudes in its locked position. Then close the door and, using the bolt as a guide, draw lines either side of it on the side of the door frame. Remember that the box that houses the bolt is wider than the bolt itself, so allow at least 3mm on either side of the bolt's width when you run these lines on to the inside of the door frame.

**14** *If you have a solid front door, fit a viewer so you can check on callers. Drill a hole through the door and screw the parts together*

Next you must measure the length from the edge to the centre of the bolt on the lock body and translate this length on to the door frame, again using a marking gauge to scribe a central line on the wood.

It now remains to drill, as before, the box hole with two consecutively-placed holes (or three at the most) using the 19mm drill bit. This done, chisel and pare away the excess wood until the finished hole is formed.

It may not be necessary to make the striking plate flush with the level of the door frame's surface—it depends on how tightly the door fits in the

frame. If it is a very close fit you must repeat the operation of holding the plate into position, scoring round it and chiselling out a recess. If there is a gap where the door meets the frame, simply screw the striking plate into position. If, however, the screw holes on the striking plate are *plunged* —punched into a slight bowl-shaped recess—you may have to countersink the holes in the door frame slightly to allow for this.

### Additional security

A good lock goes a long way to making a door secure. You can provide additional protection to the hinge edge of the door by fitting a pair of hinge bolts (fig. 12), one just below the top hinge and the other above the bottom one. Start by marking and drilling a hole in the door edge; then hammer in the reinforced bolt, and close the door so the protruding bolt marks the frame. Drill another hole at this point and fit a striking plate over it. Check that the bolts sit neatly in the holes as the door is closed.

To protect yourself from unwelcome callers, fit a door security chain (fig. 13) or a door viewer (fig. 14). Make sure that the screws securing the chain and its keeper are strong enough to prevent forcing by a would-be intruder. Viewers come in two halves which are screwed together.

# Vulnerable points around your home

**Right**: *Erect high walls or fences to deter intruders (1). Fit gates with bolts or a padlock (2). If you have to leave ladders out of doors, padlock them to stout wall brackets (3). Always lock garage doors, (4). Coat metal downpipes leading to flat roofs or upstairs windows with anti-climb paint (5). Never leave upstairs windows open (6). Make sure all doors are fitted with locks (7). Avoid strong trelliswork which a burglar could climb (8).*

**Left**: *Light shady corners where a burglar could lurk (9). Keep ground floor windows closed whenever you're out, and fit window locks where possible (10). Don't leave fanlights open. Avoid fitting extractor fans in opening casements (11). Padlock sheds and other outbuildings (12). Secure back doors with bolts on the inside, plus a mortise deadlock (13). Fit special locks and anti-lift devices to patio doors (14). Lock or bolt skylights (15).*

# FIXING FLOOR BOARDS

**Floorboard repairs are straightforward and require few special tools. But repairs are essential for safety and for preserving the good condition of the joists beneath, and the floor covering above the boards**

**Above:** *Use a strip of wood to protect the surface of the floorboards when prising out old nails*

Although solid and hardwearing, floorboard timbers are prone to all sorts of minor faults and irritations. For instance, creaks under the carpet are annoying but not dangerous; rotten boards which collapse underfoot can be dangerous as well as annoying. Even if your floorboarding is in perfect condition, it may still need work to improve draughtproofing—or to get to wiring underneath.

## Types of floorboard
Most floorboards are made of softwood—usually pine. In a single-skin floor as used in Britain, the boards are fixed at right angles to the joists which support them, and may be nailed or screwed in

place. The board ends are arranged to concide with the joists, so that the join lies over the centre of the joist, for maximum support. In a double-skin floor as used in North America, the sub-floor is usually of plywood or wafer board, but the main floorboards are still at right angles to the joists.

Floorboards fall into two basic types: square-edged, and tongue-and-grooved (fig. D). Tongued-and-grooved (T&G) boards and their derivatives are designed to eliminate draughty gaps but are more difficult to take up than their square-edged counterparts.

If you are in any doubt which of the two types is used for your flooring, choose two boards with a slight gap between them and slide a knife blade in

as far as possible—compacted grime or draughtproofing in the gap may have to be scratched out first. If the blade is stopped, the boards are either tongued or rebated.

## Lifting square-edged boards
For your starting point, choose the most convenient free end of the board you wish to lift. If the board extends right across the room and under the skirting (baseboard) on both sides, you have to start lifting it in the middle and work gradually towards the ends. When all the nails are loose, you spring the board free by pulling it upwards into a bow shape.

To lift the board, insert a bolster into the joint gap between it and the board

2 Using a piece of wood as a guide, scratch and then tease a cut with the first few teeth if you are using a tenon saw to cut on the joist

3 If you are using a padsaw or power jig saw to make a cut beside a joist, drill a small hole the width of the blade

4 Use a padsaw or compass saw to cut right across the board or, if you prefer, just to give you a slot in which to start off your handsaw

5 A padsaw can be used to sever the tongue of a tongued-and-grooved board if other forms of sawing are impracticable

6 Remove nails from the joist using a claw hammer. Protect the board alongside with an offcut. Do not hammer old nails into the joists

7 When making an extra support, start by cutting a generous length of stout timber. The extra width ensures that the board is firmly fixed

8 Mark the floorboard gap on the upper surface of the bearer. As you can see the bearer straddles the gap and acts just like the joist

9 Partly face-nail the support, to the point when the nails are just about to break through on the other side of the timber

10 Complete the nailing while pushing the bearer against the joist and upwards against the fixed boards on both sides

one end of the cutting line (fig. 3) then use a padsaw or power jig saw to cut next to, and along, the cutting line. The padsaw can be replaced with a handsaw or circular-blade power saw when convenient, and re-used if necessary at the end of the cut.

### Fitting an extra bearer

If you have removed a section of floorboard by cutting along the side of a joist, you must fit an extra bit of timber to the joist, in order to provide support for the new board end.

Make this bearer from an offcut of softwood, whose minimum dimensions ought to be no less than 38mm by 50mm. Cut it to length, slightly longer than the width of floorboarding removed and use either nails or screws for fixing it in place (fig. 9). If you choose nails, use two or three about 75mm long for each floorboard width, and hammer these partially into the broader side before positioning the bearer. If you use screws, two for each board width are enough, but drill pilot holes before fitting them.

Position the bearer against the joist and make sure that the top edges of both pieces of timber are exactly flush. Pull the bearer upwards, tightly against the floorboards on either side, while you hammer or screw it securely in place (fig. 10).

### Replacing square-edged boards

There are few problems in replacing square-edged boards. New ones of the same thickness are cut to length and—in the case of non-standard sizes—to width. If part of the board has to be tapered or otherwise shaped to fit, use the discarded board as a template when

you saw to shape the new one.

If a single board is to be replaced simply slot it into place and nail down. A number of boards covering a large area are best fitted individually—if possible in the same flooring 'pattern' as originally. No two board ends should lie side by side on the same joist.

When fitting a number of boards, do a 'dry run' first to check the width fit, and whether tight butting of the boards is possible. Where the boards are to remain visible, keep to the original spacings for the sake of appearance.

If a complete floor area is being replaced, make a point of butting all boards as tightly as possible before fixing. This is done with a floor cramp —available from hire shops—and substantially improves underfloor draught-proofing (fig. 18).

If part of the original floorboarding is to be replaced, cut off any wood which is badly split where nails were removed. Do not re-use old nail holes. These, and new holes along the length of the board, should be made good with a filler paste.

### Replacing T&G boards

Replacing tongued-and-grooved boards is not quite so straightforward. If you are re-using the old board, this can be replaced by fitting the remaining tongued or grooved side into the adjacent board. A small gap will remain on the other side—this must be plugged for complete draught-proofing.

To fit a new tongued and grooved board, you may have to plane off its tongue to get it to fit, but leave its grooved side intact.

**11** *If fitting a thicker board than the rest, a cut-out has to be made where the board crosses a joist. First mark the joist's position*

**12** *Transfer the marks from the underside of the replacement floorboard to its edges. Repeat this step at every joist position*

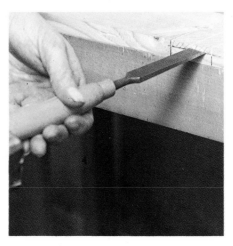

**13** *Carefully cut the board in order not to exceed the required rebate depth—this can be gauged by sight or by direct measurement*

**14** *Use a chisel to remove wood between the cutting lines. The chisel face should be down. Work in stages to end with a level cut*

**15** *Check that the rebate fits snugly and is of the required depth. Continue chiselling if the board is proud of those alongside*

If a number of adjacent boards have been removed, any necessary combination of used and new boards may be used when reflooring. The technique is to loosely fit these together over the floor area to be covered, in the process forming a low arch by making the boards slightly over-sized. Lay a spare plank over this, and press or stamp the boards down: the tongues and grooves knit together in the process. The flattened boards can then be fixed in place. Alternatively, you can use an off-cut and mallet as in fig. 17.

### Replacing short sections

If you are cutting out and replacing a short section of floorboard you may want to use up a spare piece of timber lying about the house. Alternatively, you may have difficulty getting a re- placement board which exactly matches the thickness of your existing ones. Either way, the new board will be better too thick than too thin.

Having cut your new section to length, lay it beside the gap in the floor and mark off on the underside where it is to pass over a joist. Chisel out rough rebates between the marks, to the same depth as the board is oversize (fig. 14).

When you lay the board, the rebates should fit over the joists and allow it to rest flush with the others.

### Dealing with creaking boards

Loose and creaking floorboards may be caused by incorrect nailing, by the joists below them settling, or by warp- ing and shrinkage. It is usually possible to cure a loose board simply by re- nailing or screwing it back in place.

But before you do this, check that the loose joint coincides with the centre of the joist below, taking the board up if necessary. If it does not, widen the joist with a new bearer (figs. 7-10), or replace the whole board.

To nail floorboards, use 50mm lost- head nails or flooring nails. Position them next to, and about 12mm away from, the existing nails. When you have finished, drive all the nail heads well below the surface of the board with a nail punch (nail set).

To secure floorboards with screws, use 40mm countersunk steel screws. Drill pilot holes for them 12mm from each existing nail, taking care that the holes go no deeper than the thickness of the board. When all the screws are in place, make sure that none of them protrudes above the surface.

**16** *If the replacement board is too thin, use sheet wood to make up the difference. Do not use newspaper folds for this job*

**17** *When replacing tongued boards the last two will need force before slipping into fit—use a mallet and protective wood offcut*

**18** *Nailing boards into place. A pencil line ensures accuracy. A floor cramp—worth hiring for big jobs—keeps the boards tightly packed*

**19** *If you decide to use nails for fixing a floorboard in place, hammer in the heads using a punch. Use filler and stain to conceal the hole*

**20** *If you choose to screw down a board, drill a hole to accept the screw body only. This minimizes the effort needed in fixing boards*

**21** *Use a countersink bit to drill a recess for the screw head and— if necessary—fill the hole once the board has been screwed to the joist*

# REPAIRING SKIRTING

## The purpose of skirting boards is twofold. They serve as a protective buffer at the base of walls, preserving the wall finish from abrasion, and they also act as a decorative feature

Skirting boards can be fixed to a wall in several different ways. In timber-frame construction, they are simply nailed directly through the plasterboard and into the studs, or vertical timbers, behind.

In masonry walls, nails can be hammered at an angle through the board and its backing of plaster into the brickwork (fig. A). Alternatively, strips of wood called grounds can be used. These are firmly attached to the wall and act as a fixing base for skirting boards placed over them. A continuous strip is supported at intervals by small upright pieces called soldiers (fig. B).

With either system, some plaster damage must be expected as the old skirtings are removed, and usually needs to be made good with plaster or filler before new boards are fixed.

In rare instances, the skirting is fixed to wedge-shaped uprights bedded into cavities in the brickwork (fig. C). Installed at the time the wall was made, these are held in place by a

mortar filling which often decays over a period of time. Excessive force on the skirting—such as that required to remove it—is often sufficient to dislodge these uprights. If this happens, mortar them back in. A new upright can be made by tapering a suitable length of batten.

The golden rule to bear in mind when dealing with skirting board is to be careful. The bedding plaster is easily chipped by a casual knock.

## Removing and replacing boards

To remove a length of skirting, start at one of the corners and place a bolster on the top edge where the skirting meets the wall. Using a claw hammer, hammer the bolster gently down. This will prise the skirting away from the wall at that point. Continue this action along the length

of skirting to be removed. Where greater resistance is met, the skirting will have been nailed to the wall.

With the top edge prised away from the wall you can start to remove the skirting completely. For this you need a claw hammer and a small, thin piece of plywood or hardboard to protect the wall finish. Place the claw of the hammer down behind the top edge of the board and slip the timber between the claw and the wall. Lever gently upwards on the handle, pressing the hammer head against the timber. This forces the board further away from the wall and draws out the nails at the same time.

Always use timber or a piece of hardboard to protect the wall or the hammer may leave an indent. Do not use a crowbar as this can damage the wall plaster.

Once the skirting is removed the nails should be pulled out. Use a pair of pincers to draw out the nails from the back of the board. This keeps the paint surface intact, as the face of the board often splinters if the nails are hammered through and drawn out from the front.

### Partial removal of skirting
When the area of damaged or decayed skirting is relatively small, partial replacement is more economical. Measure the length of board to be replaced and buy or make a new piece to match.

First, prise the damaged part of the board away from the wall with a bolster (fig. 1). With the top edge free, you can now insert a timber wedge between the board and the wall at the place where the first cut is to be made. The wedge should have one sloping face and be thick enough to push the board out by about 40mm. Position the wedge with the flat face to the wall so that as you hammer it down, the sloping face pushes the skirting away from the wall.

To cut out the damaged length of board, make a mitred cut at each end using a mitre block or box. There are no set rules for positioning the direction of the mitres: they can be parallel or face in opposite directions, and lean inwards or outwards.

Position the mitre block with its back against the face of the skirting and the top level with, or above the top of the skirting. If necessary, put

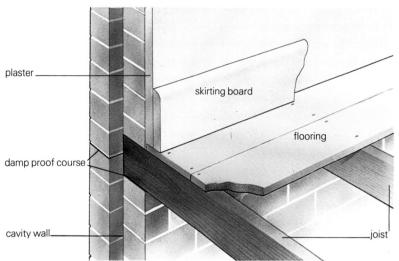

**A.** *Skirting fixed directly to the masonry. On a plastered brick wall, plaster damage usually accompanies the skirting board's removal, especially if the nails securing the board have rusted*

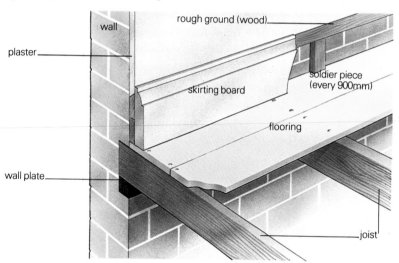

**B.** *Skirting fixed to a rough ground supported clear of the floor. Board removal may cause partial collapse of the ground and plaster base it supports*

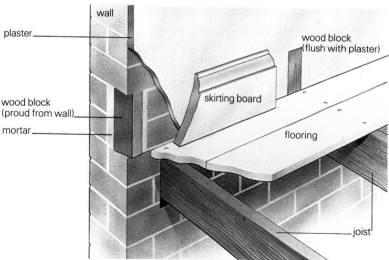

**C.** *Skirting fixed to wood blocks set in the wall at the time of building. Retaining mortar may have decayed, and both this and damp soldiers have to be made good before replacing skirting*

some suitable packing material under the block to raise it to this level. Make the first cut at the end of the damaged area using a panel saw in short rapid strokes (fig. 6). Only the first few teeth of the saw are used so these teeth must be sharp.

Continue the rapid strokes until the teeth of the saw reach the base of the block. Remove the block in order to complete the cutting down to the floor, taking great care to maintain the straight line of the cut. Pull out the wedge and reposition it where the second cut is to be made at the other end of the damaged piece of skirting. The second cut is made in the same way. Once free, lift out the piece of board from the skirting.

### Fitting the replacement board

Using the mitre block, cut a mitre at one end of the new board. Make sure that the direction of the cut is the same as that of the first cut, made when removing the damaged piece. After cutting the mitre, measure the inside edge of the area to be fitted with new skirting and transfer the measurement to the replacement board. Use the mitre block again to cut the second mitre. Check that the direction of the cut matches that in the skirting. Fit the replacement piece in the gap to check its compatability. If adjustment is necessary, use a plane with the blade set finely and remove a few shavings from the end grain.

### Fixing the replacement board

An easy method of fixing the new length of board is to use 38mm oval pins and skew nail them through the mitre joints. This way, you will nail through both thicknesses of skirting. Punch the nail heads below the surface and make good the indentations with a little woodworking filler.

Alternatively, you can use masonry nails to fix the skirting into the brickwork behind. In this case, a piece of timber the same thickness as the plaster should be placed behind to overlap the old and new pieces of skirting at each end. This ensures that the skirting will not be pushed out of its vertical position should it be knocked at the bottom.

### Matching new skirting to old

New houses usually have one of the following types of skirting: pencil round, splayed, splayed-and-rounded, or chamfered. These are easier to obtain than the elaborate older boards but fill-in pieces can be made from a square-edged board.

1 *Place a bolster behind the top edge of the skirting board. Hammer the bolster down gently. Repeat along the length of skirting*

2 *Place the claw of the hammer behind the skirting and slip the protective board between it and the wall. Lever the board away*

3 *If a board proves particularly stubborn, hammer a row of wedges down behind it. This reduces the risk of splitting the board*

4 *When the whole length of skirting has been levered from the wall, draw out the nails from the board using a pair of pincers*

5 *If a damaged length is to be removed, first drive in a wedge, then place a mitre block against the skirting while you start your cut*

6 *Now continue the cut to the bottom of the board, having first ruled a vertical pencil line to help keep the cut straight*

7 *You may have to match new board to old skirting. For a 'pencil round', mark a line 6mm from the front top edge and plane it round*

8 *For splayed skirting, mark the desired thickness on the top of the board and the end of the incline on the face. Then plane down*

9 *For splayed and rounded skirting, mark off the top of the board as for a pencil round and plane and sand the edge*

Now position the first length of board against the wall and measure from the tip of the mitre to the wall to determine the exact length. Transfer this measurement to the board and cut a square edge for the butt joint with a panel saw.

Before nailing the skirting to the wall, a replacement ground must be fitted if the old one is no longer intact or has rotted. Use masonry nails to fix the grounds into the brickwork, below the plaster (see fig. B). Mark the position of the soldiers on the floorboard below, so that you know where to nail when the skirting board has covered them. Use nails to fix the skirting to the ground support and punch the heads below the surface so that they can be filled over. It's a good idea to treat grounds and soldiers with wood preservative first.

## Internal corners

A scribed joint is used on internal angles. You cut one board to length with a square end, then cut the second to a shape that fits against the curved or moulded end of the first board. This joint is used because, unlike a mitre, it cannot open up—leaving a gap between the boards—as you nail the skirtings to the walls.

There are two ways of obtaining the scribed shape on the second board. One is to use a pair of dividers to trace the profile of one board onto the other. Then you cut out this profile with a coping saw, keyhole saw or jigsaw.

A better way is to start by fixing the first board (the square-ended one) in place. Then, on the second board, you cut a mitre. This leaves a profiled outline on the surface of the board. So you cramp the board firmly and cut around

this outline—at right angles to the board's surface—with your coping saw, keyhole saw or jigsaw. The process is easier to do than to describe or illustrate, but if you practise on an offcut first you will soon get the hang of it.

However you fix the skirting to the wall or ground, make sure the board is firmly in place—particularly where knocks are common, such as near doorways, sockets and external corners that are always in an exposed position. A firm fixing can prevent considerable additional damage to plaster and grounds that ought really to have been replaced long before they work loose.

If you are left with gaps between the skirting and the floor surface, pin lengths of slim quadrant bead to the bottom face of the boards.

21 *Cramp an offcut to this mark and set the saw blade to 45° Saw along the pencil line pressing the sole plate firmly against the offcut*

22 *Fix this board to the wall with masonry nails. Take care when hammering to avoid brickwork or plaster damage beneath*

23 *Cut a mitre on a second length of board. Measure off and cut to length, leaving a square end to go into the inside corner*

24 *Using a keyhole saw, cut along the outline on the face of the board which has been displayed by cutting the mitre first*

25 *Join the two boards with two or three nails, nailing through one mitred edge into the other. Punch the nail heads down*

26 *Measure and cut the board to length to fit over the square end of the previous length of board. To get a perfect fit, tap it down*

# REPAIRING WINDOW FRAMES

**It is essential to keep timber-framed windows in prime condition—if neglected, the wood will quickly deteriorate. And if signs of decay are left uncorrected, rot may set in**

**Below:** *Sash cords are fitted into grooves in the side of the sash and held in place by four or five clout nails. Sash cords inevitably fray through constant use and age and eventually need replacing*

A neglected window spoils the appearance of a home, causes draughts and damp, and can tempt intruders. If the signs of decay are not detected and dealt with at an early stage, further deterioration will make repair more difficult.

**Types of window**
The two basic types of timber-framed window are the casement sash (fig. C) and the double-hung sliding sash window (fig. B).

The sliding sash window operates by means of cords, pulleys and weights which counterbalance the sashes—the opening parts of the window—as they slide up and down. Two sets of beadings —thin lengths of wood—hold the

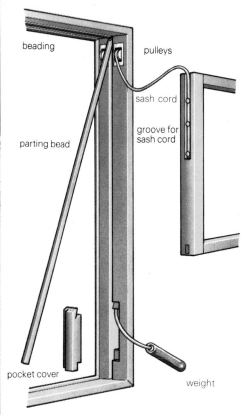

A. *Components of a sash window. The sash cord is nailed to the edge of the sash and tied to a weight*

Afterwards, remove the clout nails which hold the cords in place and—unless you intend to replace the cords—immediately tap the uppermost nails into the edges of the frame to prevent the weights on the other end of the cords from falling down behind the stile boards (fig. 6).

With both cords removed from the inner sash, you can take it from the frame and repeat the procedure for the outer one.

### Replacing sash cords

If the frame of a sash window needs attention, it is likely that the sash cords are also in a poor condition and need to be replaced. And if one of the cords has already snapped, it is possible that the others are frayed and about to break, so it is best to replace all four at the same time.

For renewing the cords, buy a slightly longer length of pre-stretched wax cord than you need to allow for waste. You will also need a lump of lead or a large nail to act as a weight for dropping the new cords down into the pockets.

Remove the sashes from the frame, as described above, and begin work on the cords of the outer sash. To get to the weights to which they are attached, unscrew the pocket covers—or lever them out if they are simply nailed or wedged into place—then pull the weights through the pocket openings and remove the cords.

Check the pulleys to make sure that they run smoothly and, if not, apply a little oil to the pivots. If the window is in particularly bad condition, the pulleys may have rusted and you will have to replace them altogether.

To fix the first new cord, tie your nail or lead weight to a piece of string about 1.5m long and feed it over the groove of the outer pulley wheel until it falls down behind the stile. Tie the new sash cord to the other end of the string and pull it over the pulley and out through the pocket opening. Now untie the string, secure the cord to the original weight and replace this inside its compartment.

Pull the weight up about 25mm and half drive a nail through the cord, into the edge of the frame to hold the weight temporarily in position. Cut the cord so that it is level with the pencil mark on the frame, made when you first removed the sashes.

Next position the outer sash so that you can fit the cord into its groove, align the end of the cord with the pencil mark on the front of the sash, then fix the cord in place with four or five clout nails. Repeat the procedure for

8 *If the mortise and tenon joints of a sash become loose, remove the sash from the frame so that you can re-assemble the joints*

10 *Knock the loose mortise and tenon joints apart, making sure that you protect the frame with a piece of waste timber*

the other cord, remove the temporary nails and lift the sash back into place within the frame.

The procedure for renewing the cords of the inner sash is almost the same but in this case pull the weights up further, almost to the pulley, before fixing the temporary nails (fig. 5).

Then replace the pocket covers, parting bead, the inner sash and then the outer beading. Grease the channels with a little candle wax to aid smooth running.

In some windows, the cord may be knotted into a hole in the side of the sash. The method of replacing is much the same, but tying the knot in exactly the right place might require some trial and error.

### Strengthening a sash

If the mortise and tenon joints of a

9 *With the glass removed from the sash frame. use a shave hook to scrape away all traces of putty from the timber*

11 *Clean all the old glue from the tenons with wire wool, then clean the area in and around the mortises with an old, blunt chisel*

12 *Having made sure that the pin and socket of each joint are clean and dry, coat the tenons with waterproof woodworking adhesive*

**13** *Slide the tenons into position, then glue replacement wedges and fit them into place. Drive them home until the joint is secure*

**14** *When all the joints have been re-assembled, check that the sash is square, then cramp it using an improvized web cramp*

sash become loose, water will eventually penetrate the gaps causing decay in the sash and possibly the surrounding timber as well. Extensive and costly repairs could then be the result of an initially minor fault.

Do not be tempted to strengthen a loose-jointed sash simply by filling the gaps. To do the job properly, remove the sash from the frame and chip away the putty holding the glass in place. Remove the glazing pins and the glass, then use a shave hook to scrape away all the remaining putty from the edges of the timber (fig. 9).

Now knock the joints apart, using a mallet with a timber offcut to protect the sash, and clean all the old glue from the tenons with wire wool. The joints in sashes are usually reinforced with two small wedges in each mortise to ensure a firm fit. Remove these and clean the inside of the mortises with an old, blunt chisel.

Using the removed wedges as a guide, mark up and cut replacements slightly longer than the originals to allow for trimming. When you have cut all the replacement wedges, coat the tenons with a waterproof woodworking adhesive and slide them into position in the mortises (fig. 12).

Tap them home with a mallet, again protecting the timber with a piece of waste wood, then apply some glue to two of your new wedges. With the angled edge of each wedge facing inwards, tap them into place with the mallet then trim off the ends with a chisel.

Fit the remaining wedges, and check that the sash frame is square by measuring the diagonals—which should be equal. Then cramp the sash. Sash cramps consist of two adjustable stops on a long bar; they come in different lengths up to 3m long with extensions. One stop is adjusted by sliding it along the bar and securing it with a pin; the other tightens like a vice jaw. Because of their size, sash cramps are expensive to buy, but they can be obtained from hire shops: this is probably a better way to get hold of them, as you are unlikely to use them very often.

Ensure that the surface of the wood does not get scratched and damaged by the action of the cramp by placing newspaper or a small block of wood between the cramp jaws and the frame. Make sure the sash is exactly square to the workpiece or distortions may result. During cramping, the bar of the sash will tend to bow in towards the workpiece, so place small wedges underneath to keep it straight while the glue is drying. Once the glue has set, you can reglaze the window and rehang the sash.

## Renewing decayed timber

If part of a sash is affected by wet rot, make a probe into the wood with a bradawl to check the extent of the damage. Providing the decayed section is small and is spread over no more than half the thickness of the rail, you can cut out the affected wood and replace it with new timber.

Knock apart the joints as described above to remove the rail which needs repair from the rest of the sash frame. Use a combination square to mark a 45° angle at each end of the decayed area (fig. 15). Then mark horizontal lines slightly below the depth of the decayed section. Make these lines on both sides of the rail.

Next, secure the timber in a vice and saw down the angled lines to the depth line with a tenon saw. Use a

keyhole saw or a jigsaw to cut along the depth line and, with the waste wood removed, smooth down the sawn edges with a bevel-edged chisel.

Use the cut piece of wood as a pattern to measure up the replacement timber, then mark the cutting lines with the combination square.

Angles of 45° are easiest cut using a mitre box to guide the saw blade, but if you do not have one, continue the cutting lines around all the faces of the timber, then secure it in a vice and cut the replacement section. Plane down the sawn edges of the new wood and check its fit in the sash rail. If it is slightly oversize on any of its faces, sand down the unevenness.

The replacement wood is fixed into place by two or three screws, countersunk below the surface. Drill holes in the new section for these, staggering them slightly, then apply some glue to the underside and angled faces and cramp the section into place. Extend the screw holes into the sash rail to a depth of at least 12mm, drive in the screws and sink their heads well below the surface of the wood.

When the glue has set, remove the cramp and plane down the surfaces of the new wood until it is flush with the surrounding timber. Then reassemble the sash as described above.

## Sticking windows

Apart from the faults already described, casements and sashes can stick because of a build-up of old paint or because the timber in the frame swells slightly.

The former problem is easily solved by removing the offending frame, stripping off all the old paint and then repainting. But swelling is a problem which can come and go with the weather. On casement windows, where it occurs most often, swelling can usually be allowed for by adjusting the casement hinges—a far less drastic solution than planing off the excess.

Mark the swollen part of the casement and judge whether increasing or decreasing the depth of one of the hinge recesses will bring it away from the window frame.

To increase the depth, pare away 2mm or so of wood from the recess with a sharp chisel. Try the casement for fit again before you start to remove any more.

To decrease the depth, cut a shim of cardboard or thin hardboard to the shape of the recess and fix it in place with a dab of glue. Punch or drill screw holes through the shim then replace the casement. Do this with great care to ensure a proper fit.

**1** To cure a loose or creaking tread test the wedges glued into place beneath. Remove any wedges that are loose or damaged

**2** If a wedge is warped or damaged, cut a replacement. Make the new wedge the same shape but about 20mm longer

off any old, hardened glue and reglue it in place.

When all the wedges are secure, check the glue blocks (where fitted) and remove any loose ones. If screw fixing holes into the stairs have become enlarged, plug them before refitting the blocks. If the blocks have been nailed, it is worth replacing the nails with No. 8 (4.2mm) 32mm screws. Remove any hardened glue and make sure the surfaces are clean and dry before you reglue loose blocks.

If there are no blocks secure any loose treads by fixing metal brackets, a little shorter than the treads, 150mm in from each string (fig. 7).

**Covered stairs**

If the underside of the affected part of the stairs is covered with lath and plaster, access can be gained only by ripping out the plaster with a claw hammer and bolster. This is a time consuming and extremely dirty job, but worthwhile if the treads are particularly loose.

**3** Use an old chisel to chip out all the old adhesive in the housing. Make sure that both the housing and the wedge are clean and dry

**4** Coat the edges of the new wedge with some woodworking adhesive. Push the wedge upwards into place in its housing

Fortunately, a loose tread can often be secured—though less effectively—from above. The joints between the top edges of the risers and the treads are sometimes held together by screws or nails. These may have become loose and need retightening.

Where no screws or nails are fitted, there may be a considerable gap between the treads and the top edges of the risers. New screws can be fixed if the treads are butt-jointed. In tongued-and-grooved joints use nails, as the slender parts of the wood in the joint might be weakened by screws.

To identify the type of joint, insert a knife blade into the gap between the tread and the riser. Where there is a

**5** Drive the wedge with a hammer to make sure that it fits tightly. Hold a timber offcut against the wedge to prevent it from slipping

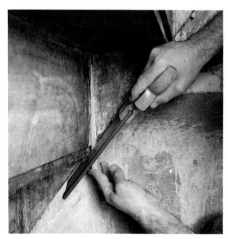

**6** When the wedge is secure in the housing, leave it until the glue has set, then trim off the end with a tenon saw

**7** If there are no glue blocks under the steps, secure loose treads by fixing metal brackets about 150mm in from each string

moulded strip beneath the nosing, prise this off with an old chisel first. If the knife blade goes right through, it is a butt joint; if its path is blocked it is tongued-and-grooved. In some tongued-and-grooved joints the outside edge of the riser forms the front of the tongue, so there is no horizontal gap between the two.

To secure a butt-jointed tread, drill pilot holes for two countersunk screws through its top surface and into the riser, just behind the nosing. Position the holes about 150mm in from each string. Having countersunk the holes and driven in the screws, fill over the screw heads with wood filler. If the stairs are not carpeted, match the wood filler with the existing wood.

The steps of open-riser staircases, which are a feature of open-plan architecture, have no risers, giving them a modern airy look. The treads can be supported on wooden blocks attached to the inside faces or the top edges of the strings, or they can be fitted into housings cut into the sides of each string.

The treads of an open-riser seldom creak, because of their thickness and the more simple structure of the staircase. However, if they are housed into the strings, wood shrinkage may cause the treads to move in the housings.

If a housed tread creaks or can be felt to move, push it up in its housings from below and cut wedges to the rough shape of the areas in which movement is taking place. Coat the wedges with PVA adhesive and drive them firmly into the housings below the tread with a timber offcut and a hammer. Then, if possible, allow 24 hours before stepping on any newly wedged treads.

On some open-risers, a steel rod is fixed between the strings beneath every fourth or fifth tread. If treads seem loose, tighten the mounting screws of these rods.

## Worn nosings

On old, uncarpeted stairs, years of use inevitably wear away the nosings—particularly in the middle. If a nosing is badly worn, it can be dangerous and should be replaced.

Prise off the moulded strip beneath the nosing (if fitted) and on a cut-string staircase, prise off the planted side nosing as well. Use a firmer chisel or a jig saw to cut back the edge of the nosing to an angle, then level the surface with a block plane (fig. 11). Do not cut the wood right back to the riser or the joint may be weakened, particularly if it is of the tongued-and-grooved type.

**8** *If a nosing is badly worn, it can be dangerous. To replace a nosing mark out the area that is to be cut away from the tread*

**10** *Do not cut the wood right back to the riser or the joint with the tread may be weakened. Remove the cut section from the tread*

Next, cut a piece of 38mm x 32mm softwood to the length of the exposed tread—on a cut-string, allow extra length for the mitre into the planted nosing—and then glue and nail it into place. When the glue has set, use a block plane again to shave the new piece to shape (fig. 16).

Where necessary, mitre the end of the new piece so that if fits with the edge of the planted nosing. If you want to make the new nosing more secure, fit countersunk screws and fill the ends with wood filler.

## Worn treads

If the wear extends further back from the nosing, you càn use a plane or chisel to level the surface. But bear in mind that if you remove more than 5mm of wood, you may seriously weaken the tread.

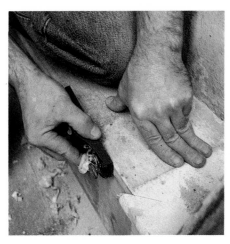

**9** *Cut out the affected part of the nosing with a jig saw or a firmer chisel with a wide blade. Mitre the cut at each end*

**11** *Level the surface that has been cut with a block plane, then use a chisel to clean out any remaining fibres in the corners*

**12** *Cut a new piece of nosing, to the length of the area, from a piece of 38mm x 32mm softwood. Hold into place and check for fit*

**13** *Hammer the new length into place protecting it with an offcut of timber, then mark the shape of the nosing onto its edges*

A better alternative is to remove the nosing as above and fill the worn areas with a strong wood filler so that the surface is level. When the filler is dry, cut a piece of 6mm plywood to the shape of the tread and glue and pin it in place. Fit a new nosing to match the modified tread.

## Loose newel posts
It is unusual for newel posts to cause any problems when securely fixed but if one becomes loose, it should be dealt with immediately as it is such a vital part of the structure.

To secure a loose post, first lift the adjacent floorboards (see pages 43-48). Tighten the bolts that attach the post to the floor joist and, if possible, reinforce the joint between the two by screwing wood blocks or metal angle brackets to the corners.

If the mortise-and-tenon joint between a newel post and the outer string is loose, the treads and risers can also work themselves loose, making the whole staircase potentially dangerous.

Use a 9.5mm drill to bore two holes into one side of the newel post, through the string tenon, and into the other side of the post. Prepare two hardwood dowels, 10mm longer than the holes, and coat them with PVA adhesive. Insert the dowels into the holes then, once the glue has set, trim the dowels so that they are flush.

The bottom step of a staircase—called the *curtail* step—often projects beyond the newel post and is separate from the rest of the structure. If it is badly worn, it can be replaced entirely, though you should make sure that the replacement is exactly the same height and width as

**14** *Remove the new piece and, using the marks on its ends as a guide, plane it roughly to the shape of the existing nosings*

**15** *Apply woodworking adhesive to the new nosing and drive it back into place. Nail the new nosing and punch the heads below the surface*

the old step or the altered slope may cause an accident.

If any other tread is particularly badly worn, or even cracked, do not attempt to replace it without first seeking professional advice. Where the treads and risers are tongued-and-grooved, or where a rough carriage is fitted, it is virtually impossible to remove a tread without dismantling the entire staircase.

However, where the underneath of the staircase is accessible, a cracked tread can be strengthened satisfactorily by fitting angled brackets at each side as shown in fig. 7.

## Loose balusters and handrails
If the balusters are fitted into recesses at either end, they are unlikely to come loose. Often, however, they are cut at an angle at the top and just

nailed to the handrail. Where the lower side of the handrail is grooved, the spaces between the balusters are often filled by strips of wood glued and pinned into place.

To remove a loose baluster, prise out any filler pieces under the handrail and tap the top of the baluster in the upward direction of the staircase. If the baluster is fitted into a mortise at the other end, it should now be possible to pull it away. On a cut-string staircase, prise off the planted nosing and tap the baluster base out from the edge of the stairs.

With the baluster removed, clean both ends and glue a short block of wood on to the top edge. When the glue is dry, cut the block to the shape of the baluster and test it for fit between the rail and string. Trim the block to the correct length to make a

**16** *Once the adhesive has set, use a block plane to shape the profile of the new nosing accurately. Then smooth the edge with glasspaper*

tight fit, then glue it back into place and replace any wood filling strips and the planted nosing, if fitted.

To secure a loose wall handrail, either fix longer plugs and screws to the loose brackets, or reposition the brackets and fill the old holes. Some people are tempted to remove the handrail altogether, but in some circumstances this is forbidden in the UK Building Regulations.

The handrail between newel posts, is either attached by mortise-and-tenon joints, or glued and nailed to the posts. Joints can be reinforced in the same way as those between the newel posts and outer strings, or, if the handrail is glued, fresh glue and new nails can be added. But if a handrail is loose, and the balusters are in a bad condition as well, it may be worth replacing the whole assembly.

# Timber staircase construction

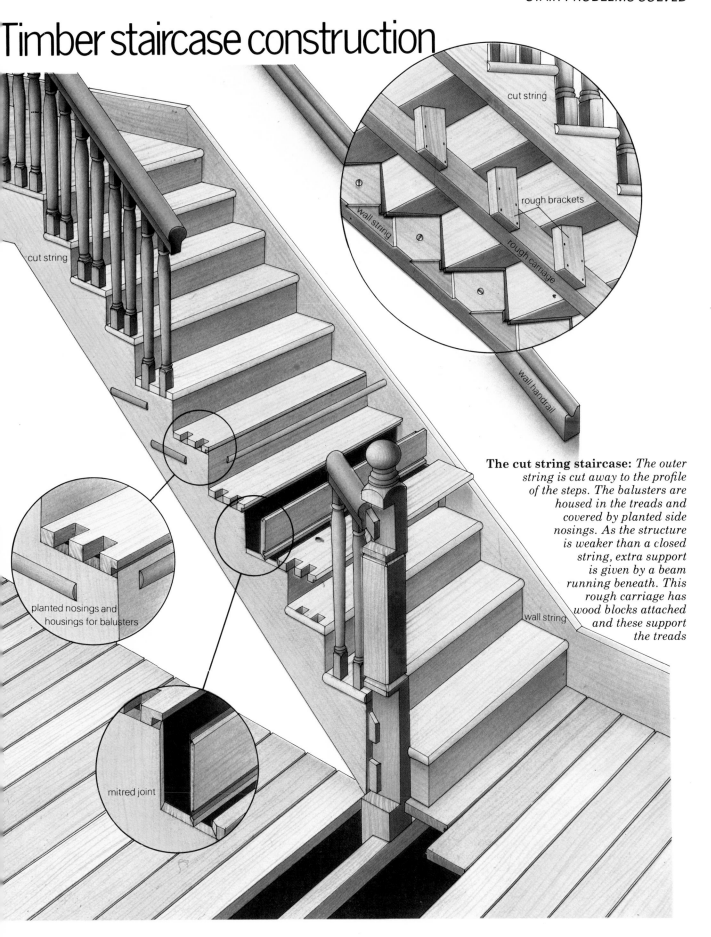

cut string

rough brackets

wall string

rough carriage

wall handrail

cut string

planted nosings and housings for balusters

mitred joint

wall string

**The cut string staircase:** *The outer string is cut away to the profile of the steps. The balusters are housed in the treads and covered by planted side nosings. As the structure is weaker than a closed string, extra support is given by a beam running beneath. This rough carriage has wood blocks attached and these support the treads*

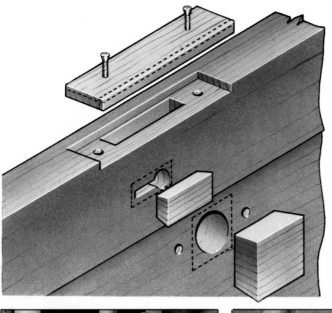

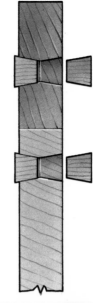

**A. Left:** *Holes left in the frame by relocating the lock, keyhole and handle need to be filled with wood*

## Cutting out

The hinge recesses are now ready to be cut out. Use a bevel-edged chisel and start by chopping downwards across the grain in a series of cuts 5–6mm apart (fig. 6). Leave a thin uncut border of about 2–3mm around the three edges (fig. 6). Hold the chisel flat, bevel side up, and pare away the chipped-up timber. Finally, with the flat side of the chisel parallel to the door edge, clean out the recess.

The hinge should now press firmly into place flush with the surrounding timber. You may have trouble with some types of hinges which are bent due to pressure in their manufacture. If

**1** *Before fixing hinges, stand the door on edge and support it securely with a vice firmly clamped to one end of the door*

**2** *Position the hinges 215mm from the top of the door and 225mm from the base, keeping them well clear of any joints*

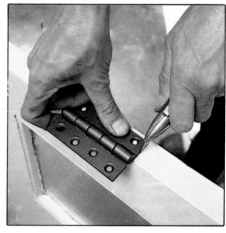

**3** *Use a marking knife to mark the hinge position on the door edge. Make sure that the hinge knuckle is facing the right way.*

**4** *Then set a marking gauge to the width of a hinge leaf and scribe this on the door edge between the two lines previously marked*

**5** *Reset your marking gauge to the depth of one hinge leaf and mark this on to the face of the door frame between the two knife cuts*

**6** *Use a bevel-edged chisel to cut out the hinge recesses. Make a number of cuts 5-6mm apart, to leave an uncut border around the edge*

this is the case, pare away a further 1–2mm from the recess.

## Fixing hinges

Once the hinge is comfortably in position, carefully mark the screw holes with a sharp pencil then remove the hinge and remark the screw centres with a centre punch. Try to mark these a little off centre—towards inside of the recess—so that once the screws are inserted, the hinge will be pulled snugly into position (fig. 8).

Drill pilot holes to the depth of the screws and then clearance holes deep enough for the screw shanks. For heavy butt hinges use No. 7 or No. 8 × 38mm screws. Insert the screws so that they finish level with or slightly below the hinge plate (fig. 9).

If you are using brass screws, put in a steel screw first. This will cut a thread in the wood and avoid the possibility of shearing off or damaging the soft brass screw heads.

## Fitting the door

Position the door in its frame by supporting the base with wooden wedges made from offcuts (fig. 10). Both door and hinges should be in the fully open position unless you are using rising butt hinges, in which case they should be closed.

With all types of hinge, make an allowance at the base of the door for any proposed floor covering and adjust the gap as necessary by altering the positions of the wedges. When you are satisfied that the door is in the right place, mark the position of the top and bottom of each hinge on the door frame with a pencil.

With the door removed from the frame, mark out the hinge recesses—

their length, width and depth—accurately with a marking knife and adjustable try square. Use the same technique to cut the recesses as you used for those on the door.

Replace the door and position it exactly using the wooden wedges, then tap the hinge leaves into place in the waiting recesses. Finally, mark and pre-drill each screw hole, then insert one screw in each hinge so that you can check that the door opens and closes properly. If it sticks at any point, make minor adjustments by chiselling away more of the rebates before you drive home the remaining screws.

## Sticking doors

If a door sticks and you can find nothing wrong with the hinges, it may be that part of the door frame has swollen. Where the swelling is slight and there is plenty of clearance between door and frame, investigate the possibility of bringing the swollen part away from the frame by either packing or deepening one of the hinge recesses. Be sure to make only the slightest adjustments in one go, or the door may stick elsewhere around the frame.

Where the swelling is more severe, you have no choice but to plane off the excess and redecorate the door. The planing can be done with the door in situ providing you first wedge the base to take the weight off the hinges.

Older doors and those particularly exposed to damp may warp or become loose at the joints, causing them to fit badly in their frames. In the case of

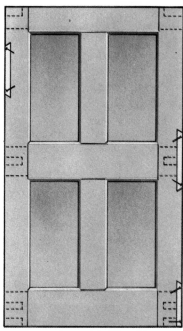

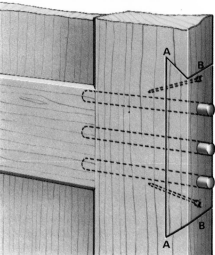

**B. Right:** *Badly weakened areas need to be cut out and replaced with dowelled sections. Start by cutting along line A-A, then B-A*

7 *Cut out the chipped-out timber in the hinge recesses with a chisel —held bevel side up—until the recess is clean and smooth*

8 *Mark the screw holes slightly off centre towards the inside of the recesses. This allows the hinge to bed securely once it is fixed*

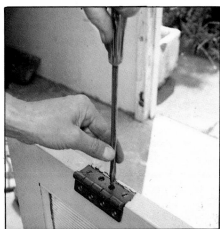

9 *Once you have drilled pilot and clearance holes, insert the screws so that they are slightly below the level of the hinge plates*

**Dealing with rattling doors**

A rattling door is usually an indication that the timber has shrunk and the door no longer butts tightly up against the door stop. You may be able to cure the rattle with self-adhesive draughtproofing foam, but a better remedy is to reposition the striker plate on the door frame so it is a little nearer the door stop. This involves unscrewing the striker plate, enlarging it slightly and fixing it, using new screw holes.

If the door has also warped slightly along its opening edge and cramping is not effective in pulling it back square, the best solution is to mark the profile of the warped door edge on the door stop and then prise it off so you can plane it down to the line. Replace it so its planed edge meets the door surface snugly, then fill the nail heads and repaint the bare wood to complete the repair.

**18** Close the door and measure the gap between the door and stop. Then mark this distance on the frame, measured from the edge of the striker

**19** Unscrew the countersunk screws holding the striker plate in place along the door frame. Set the striker plate and screws aside

**20** Use a straightedge (or the striker plate itself if you prefer) and a marking knife to indicate the edge of the new striker plate rebate

**21** Next use a sharp bevel-edged chisel to enlarge the rebate up to the marked line. You may have to enlarge the latch and lock recesses

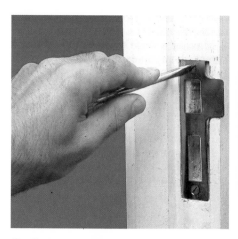

**22** Test the fit of the striker plate, then screw it into position and test the operation of the door. Finally, fill the exposed edge of the old rebate

**23** If the door is warped and cannot be cramped square, reshape the door stop. Scribe the profile of the door edge onto the stop

**24** Lever the bottom edge of the stop away from the frame, starting at the bottom and working upwards. Pull out all old nails

**25** Cramp the stop in a vice and plane the edge down to the marked line. Then nail it back to the door frame so the door fits against it

# REPAIRING GUTTERS AND DOWNPIPES

**Gutters and downpipes play a vital role in protecting your house from the effects of rain. But unless guttering is regularly maintained it will deteriorate, causing leaks or overflows. The damp in turn causes structural damage which often costs a fortune to repair**

All guttering systems should be inspected twice a year, in late autumn and again in the spring. It will almost certainly be necessary to sweep out any accumulation of leaves and dirt with a hand brush and trowel or, in the case of plastic guttering, with a shaped piece of hardboard.

Keep the debris well away from the outlet leading to the down pipe. If the outlet does not have a cage or grille fixed to prevent debris from entering and blocking the downpipe, roll a piece of galvanized wire netting into a ball and insert it in the neck of the pipe. Do make sure that the wire ball is sufficiently large not to fall down the pipe.

With cast-iron or galvanized iron guttering, check carefully for any rust. Use a wire brush to remove loose flakes of paint and rust and treat the surface with a rust inhibitor. The surface should then be given one or two coats of bituminous paint to form a strong protective layer.

On Ogee-section guttering (fig. A), or galvanized guttering fixed on with through spikes, rust may well be found around the fixings to the fascia—in which case the damaged section may have to be removed for treatment on the ground.

## Basic safety
In order to reach the gutters for a close inspection, you will have to rig up some form of access and in most cases this means using a ladder. If you haven't already got a ladder, you shouldn't have any trouble in hiring one from your local tool hire shop.

When using a ladder, it's as well to be aware of a few basic safety rules. First, don't lean the ladder against the guttering itself or the fascia which may not be able to take the weight. If you can, hire a ladder stand-off which clips to the rungs and holds the ladder away from the wall. Secondly, make sure that the foot of the ladder stands square and firm on the ground—the base should be placed out from the wall by a quarter of its height. And thirdly, never work from the very top of a ladder—you'll have nothing to hold on to and it's easy to lose balance.

**Left**: *Clearing a downpipe. A blockage in a downpipe can cause the system to overflow with damaging results*

1 *Leaves and debris soon accumulate in gutters, especially during the autumn. Clean them out with a trowel or stiff brush*

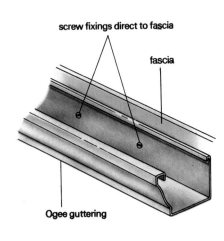

screw fixings direct to fascia

fascia

Ogee guttering

**A.** *Guttering of Ogee-section is often screwed directly to the fascia boards*

## Sagging gutters

If a gutter sags, water may overflow or the joints may crack and leak. A bucket of water poured in at the highest point of the system reveals any such defects.

The commonest causes of sagging are broken or bent brackets, or loose fixing screws or spikes. Most guttering is supported on brackets screwed either to the fascia boards underneath the eaves of the roof (fig. C) or to the ends of the roof rafters.

To rectify a sagging gutter, remove the defective sections and examine the brackets to see if they are firmly fixed. If they are not, use longer screws to secure them. Where brackets are bent or corroded, replace them with matching new ones.

Replacing a rafter bracket (fig. D) normally involves removing the roof covering directly above it, though this problem can often be overcome by fixing a fascia bracket adjacent to the faulty rafter bracket to give the necessary extra support.

Ogee section guttering differs from other types in that it is screwed or spiked directly on to the fascia. Sagging here is usually caused by the fixing devices rusting and then pulling away from the fascia. In this case, plug the holes and re-fasten with new screws or spikes.

A common fault with guttering occurs where the slope or fall towards the downpipe outlet becomes distorted —because of faulty installation or settlement of the house itself. Too steep a fall causes water to overflow at the downpipe outlet. Too shallow a fall results in a build up of water and sediment along the run.

To determine the correct fall for an incorrectly aligned section, tie a length of twine along the top of the gutter—from the high end to the out-flow point—and use it as a guide to reposition the intervening supports. The gutter should fall 25mm for every 3m of its length.

## Leaking joints in cast-iron

The joints in cast-iron gutter systems are held together by nuts and bolts which are usually screw-headed. A proprietary sealing compound—often a mixture of putty and red lead or a mastic sealer—is sandwiched between the two ends to make the joint water-tight (fig. D).

A leaking joint may be patched up by cleaning the area with a wire brush and applying one or two coats of bituminous paint. However, for a more permanent repair the section on one side of the leaking joint must be removed, cleaned and replaced. If the removed piece is in the middle of a run, two new joints have to be made—one at each end of the section.

Start by removing the bolts which hold the joints together. These may well have rusted and seized—in which case apply penetrating oil to loosen them. If this fails, saw through the bolts with a junior hacksaw. With Ogee-section guttering, remove the screws holding the section to the fascia as well.

Lift out the loosened section—making sure as you do so that its weight does not catch you off balance —and take it to the ground (fig. 3). Returning to the guttering, chip off all traces of old sealing compound from the hanging end (fig. 4) and scour it thoroughly with a wire brush. Repeat the cleaning operation on the removed section (figs. 5 and 6).

Apply fresh sealing compound to the socket section of the joint, spreading it in an even layer about 6mm

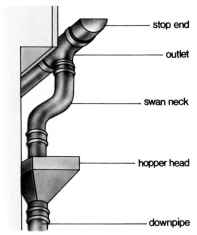

stop end

outlet

swan neck

hopper head

downpipe

**B.** *This downpipe connects to the gutter run via a swan neck*

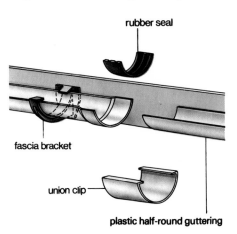

rubber seal

fascia bracket

union clip

plastic half-round guttering

**C.** *A section held by a fascia bracket. This joint type is sealed in the socket*

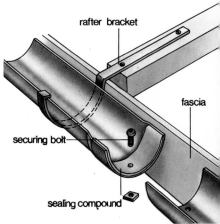

rafter bracket

fascia

securing bolt

sealing compound

**D.** *A joint in cast-iron guttering. The gutter is supported by rafter brackets*

2 This leaking section of cast-iron guttering is on the end of a run. The guttering is secured by screws in the fascia rather than by brackets

3 When the bolt in the joint at the other end of the section has been loosened and removed, you can pull the section away from the wall

4 The leak is at the joint with the adjoining section. Using hammer and screwdriver, gently chip off traces of old sealing compound

5 Repeat the cleaning operation for the section that has been removed. Scrape off old sealing compound from the joint end

6 When the old sealing compound has been removed, scour clean the two ends of the joint thoroughly with a wire brush

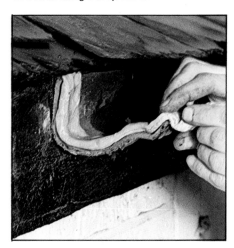

7 Apply new sealing compound to the socket section of the joint, spread in an even layer about 6mm thick over the socket area

8 Having replaced the removed section and fitted the joint together, take a new bolt and insert it in the hole in the joint from above

9 Screw the securing nut onto the end of the bolt and tighten with screwdriver and spanner so that joint closes and squeezes out compound

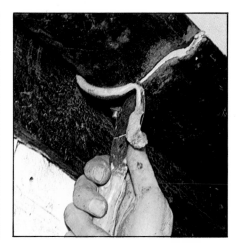

10 Use a putty knife to trim away all excess sealing compound squeezed onto the surface above and below the gutter

**17** *Hopper heads are notorious for collecting leaves and rubbish. Lift out as much loose debris as possible—try not to push it down*

**18** *Force out a blockage in a straight downpipe with a stout rod. If there is a bend in the pipe, try pulling out the blockage with wire*

**19** *Wash out any residue with a strong jet of water from a garden hose. To prevent further blockages, cover with mesh*

## Replacing an enamelled section

Gutters made from thin-section aluminium or galvanized steel, finished with white baked-on enamel, are less subject to rust than cast-iron gutters. But they are apt to dent sometimes just by your leaning a ladder against them.

The procedure for replacing a damaged section is much the same as for plastics. First, jam a block of wood inside the gutter while you draw the fixing spikes with a claw hammer, and disconnect the damaged section at the nearest joints. Cut the new section with a hacksaw, using the old one to measure the correct length, and file off the burrs on the cut edges. If you are using spike supports, drill holes through the new section to receive them.

Next, clean off the old sealing compound from the undamaged sections, as described above. Fill the joint connectors with sealing compound, slip them into place, and fit the new gutter section, spiking it into place. Finally, bend over into the gutter the top ends of the connectors if these are designed with fold-over tabs.

At external corners, as with other types of gutter, you need two fixing spikes—one into each length of fascia.

## Clearing blocked downpipes

Before unblocking a downpipe, put a plastic bowl or large tin under the base of the pipe at the discharge into the drain to prevent any debris entering the drainage system.

When cleaning hopper heads (fig. B), use rubber gloves to protect your hands against sharp edges.

To clear a blockage in a straight downpipe, tie a rag firmly to one end of a long pole and poke it down the pipe. Once the blockage has been dislodged, flush the pipe thoroughly with a hose.

If the downpipe is fitted with a hopper head carefully clear by hand any debris which has collected. Try not to compress the debris, or it may cause further blockage in the downpipe.

With plastic hopper heads, wipe the inside with a cloth and soapy water once the debris has been cleared.

With some systems, the guttering is positioned some way out from the wall and water is directed into the downpipe through an angled section known as a *swan neck* (fig. B). To clear a blockage here, use a length of fairly stiff wire in place of the pole so that the bends may be negotiated. With wire it's best to pull out debris.

If a blockage is beyond reach, the lower part of the downpipe will have to be dismantled.

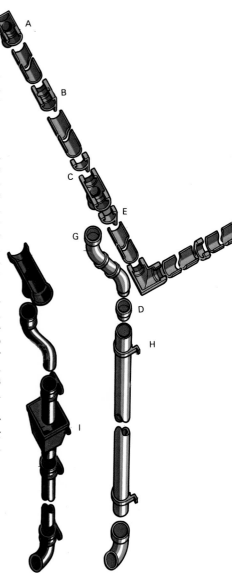

**H.** *Modern rainwater systems are nearly always made from plastic which doesn't rot and last virtually indefinitely. The weak points in a plastic system are the joints but in most cases it is possible to buy and install replacements. The sections that you are most likely to have to replace include the following.* **A.** *Stop-end outlet.* **B.** *Coupling clip.* **C.** *Running outlet.* **D.** *Angle piece.* **E.** *Support bracket.* **F.** *Stop-end.* **G.** *Three-piece swan neck.* **H.** *Downpipe bracket. When buying replacement parts, check that they are compatible with the existing system.*

*Old cast-iron rainwater systems (inset) usually follow a different plan in that they have hopper heads to collect the water that drains from the gutter. Because cast iron is heavy and corrodes easily, the weak points are often to be found around the support brackets* **(I)** *which have pulled away from the wall*

# REPOINTING BRICKWORK

**Left:** *Repointing is essential to protect the brickwork if the old mortar is crumbling or missing*

## The mortar joints in brickwork protect a wall from the damaging effects of rainwater. So if the mortar shows signs of decay, replace it with fresh mortar to make a new seal

As long as brickwork is correctly designed and well built, it does not require much in the way of maintenance or repair work. But, as a building ages, the mortar joints between the bricks may begin to decay and crumble. Flaking joints in brickwork allow water to penetrate the wall and should never be neglected. The remedy for crumbling joints is repointing—clearing out the old mortar a short way and replacing it with fresh mortar to make a new waterproof seal.

### Types of joint

The mortar between bricks can be finished in one of several ways; wherever possible, you should try to match new joints to the existing ones. However, if the old mortar is particularly badly decayed, you may not be able to see what type of joint has been used. In this case it is worthwhile making new weather-struck joints (fig. C).

The horizontal joints of this type have sloped surfaces which are slightly recessed below the upper brick and slightly overhanging the lower one. This slope allows water to run off quickly and prevents it from lodging on the lower edge of the joints, thus giving the wall further protection from rain and moisture. The vertical joints slope from one side to the other and match the angle of the horizontals above and below. Other types of joint commonly used in brickwork include:

**Flush joint:** When the mortar has almost dried, it is rubbed over with a piece of wood or old sacking to produce a surface flush with the surrounding brickwork (fig. E). This type of pointing looks particularly effective when used in conjunction with smooth-surfaced bricks.

**Keyed or round joint:** This is produced by running along the surface of the mortar with a semi-circular piece of metal to form a shallow, curved depression (fig. B).

**Recessed joint:** This is formed by scraping out the freshly-laid mortar to a depth of about 6mm below the brick surface, then smoothing the surface of the remaining mortar with a piece of wood the width of the joint (fig. D). Recessed joints look best on rough-textured bricks but should be used only where they match the existing pointing. If used on external walls in cold climates, the bricks must be hard and durable, otherwise water may collect and freeze on the ledges causing pieces of brick to flake off.

### Equipment

For repointing brickwork, even if you are working over quite a small area of wall, you need a spot board on which to mix the mortar and a hawk for carrying the mortar to the work area (refer to page 73). For applying the mortar to the joints you need a pointing trowel, which resembles a small bricklayer's trowel, and for clearing out the old mortar use a shave hook with its pointed end cut off square.

If you are constructing weather-struck joints, you also need a *frenchman* for trimming away the excess mortar at the bottom of the horizontal joints. A suitable frenchman can be made from an old kitchen knife. Use a hacksaw to cut off the end of the knife, smooth off any burrs around the cut with a file, then heat the tip and bend it into a right-angle about 12mm from the end.

To guide the frenchman neatly along the joints when trimming, you need a straight-edged piece of timber which is held immediately below the top edge of the lower brick. Attach two pieces of hardboard to each end of the piece of wood so that when it is held against the wall, there is a slight gap allowing the trimmed mortar to fall through (fig. A).

Wherever possible, the mortar for repointing should be mixed to match the composition of the existing mortar. If you do not know the mixing proportions of the original mortar, use a 1:1/2:4 1/2 (cement:lime:sand) mix or 1 part of masonry cement to 3 parts of sand. An exception to the rule is the softer type of facing brick, where you should use a weaker mix; a proportion of 1:1:6 is more appropriate here.

Use as fine a grade of soft sand as possible, also called builders' or bricklayers' sand.

silicate bricks, lightly abrade the surface with a brick of the same colour to remove large pieces.

If marks still remain on the brickwork because the mortar has penetrated the surface, they can be removed with a very dilute solution of hydrochloric acid—1:10 by volume for clay bricks and 1:2 by volume for calcium silicate. Saturate the brickwork with clean water, then apply the solution sparingly with an old paint brush, taking great care not to get any on your skin or in your eyes. When the area has been thoroughly treated, hose down the brickwork to remove every trace. The surface of some types of brick can be affected by acid so, if in doubt, consult the brick manufacturer before embarking on treatment of this kind.

### Colouring joints

To produce a matching or decorative effect in finished brickwork vegetable dyes, proprietary colourants and spe-

*A. To trim the excess mortar from the bottom of the weather-struck joints, use a frenchman and draw it along the top edge of a straight length of timber held just below the top edge of the lower brick. Attach a thin block of wood to each end of the timber to let the trimmed mortar fall through the gap. Make a frenchman from an old kitchen knife*

cial coloured cements are all available from builders' merchants and can be added to the mortar mix if desired. But because the colour will be altered by the texture of ordinary sand, you should use white sand in the mix, if possible. Remember also that cement with colour additives requires less water than is normally used.

If you use a vegetable dye, the final colour will be a lighter shade as the colour pales as the mortar dries; experiment first with small measured quantities of mortar and dye and allow them to dry out. When you have obtained the required shade in one of the experimental batches, mix up your first full batch and add the dye in an equal proportion.

If you are repointing part of a wall and want the colour of the fresh mortar to match that in the existing joints, rub the joints around the area with candlewax to prevent them from absorbing the colouring in the new mortar mixture.

*B. Keyed joints are formed by smoothing the surface of the mortar with a rounded piece of metal*

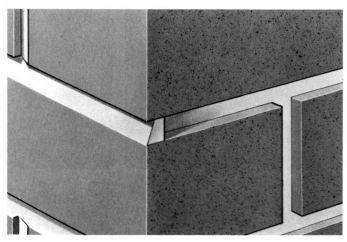

*C. The slope of weather-struck joints allows water to run off quickly, protecting the wall from rain*

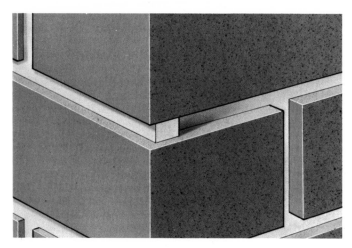

*D. The mortar in recessed joints is scraped out to a depth of about 6mm below the brick surface*

*E. Flush joints are produced by rubbing the mortar with a piece of wood to form a smooth surface*

# INSTALLING A ROOF WINDOW

● **Planning a roof window conversion** ● **Window designs** ● **Tools and equipment** ● **Preparatory work** ● **Marking out and cutting an opening** ● **Fixing the window in place** ● **Fixing U-type and L-type flashings**

**Below:** *Installing a roof window is an economical and practical way of adding light and ventilation, enabling you to open up space in the home—such as a loft or attic—which might otherwise go to waste*

Parts of the home like the space under the roof are often under used—simply because of the lack of light or ventilation. Installing a roof window gets around these problems and enables you to create an extra room with a minimum amount of work—without the need for major structural alterations to the house.

Although roof windows are most usually fitted in attics, their use is by no means restricted to the main roof of the house. They can just as easily be installed in garage, shed or extension roofs providing the pitch of the roof is somewhere between 20° and 85° and the timbers are sound.

## Planning a roof window

You will almost certainly need building regulations approval for a roof window —this means drawing up plans of your proposals and submitting them to your local council. You may also need permission under the planning regulations, which are different from building regulations: see the panel overleaf for details.

If you simply want to introduce more light and ventilation into an attic which is already used as a room, then obtaining the necessary permissions is relatively straightforward. But if you want to convert an ordinary attic into a habitable room the procedure is more extensive. From the planning point of view, you will be creating an extension, which may or may not require planning permission. From the building regulations point of view, you will have to make sure the attic will satisfy the regulations for a habitable room—for

**11** *Next fit the bottom flashing section into place and secure it by slotting the bottom profile over the top and screwing it tight*

**12** *Next fit the side flashings and secure them by adjusting the sliding clips so that they can be nailed into one of the battens*

**13** *To support the top flashing, fill the gap above the frame with battens spaced at 20mm intervals and nailed across the rafters*

**14** *Then slide the top and side profiles into position and fix them securely with screws to the frame below*

**15** *Finally, clip the top flashing into place and make sure that it is firmly attached to the top profile you have just fitted*

**16** *Check all connections for tightness and then dress the bottom flashing—made of pliable lead—against the roof covering*

## Preparatory work

Although all of the work involved in installing a roof window can be safely carried out from inside, it is very easy to drop tiles and timber on unsuspecting passers-by. So, before you start work, cordon off the area immediately below where you are working with clearly marked signs and improvized barriers.

If fitting the window involves cutting away rafters, prepare for this before you start work. To support the ends of each severed rafter, make up two pieces of timber long enough to stretch from the floor and cut the top ends at an angle to fit the rafter slope at top and bottom.

Once the rafters are cut through, timber noggins—called trimmers—of the same dimensions as the existing rafters are fixed at top and bottom across the gap to strengthen the frame. Prepare for this by measuring the distance between rafters that will accommodate the width of the window.

Next, unpack the window and remove the wooden sash by rotating it through 180° as if you were opening it. This will expose the hinges so that you can fully tighten the retaining screws and lift the frame away.

Strip the sash free of all metal components except for the two aluminium profiles near the hinge—most can be screwed loose then pulled free. Check that all the woodwork is clean and free of defects then give it a protective coat of polyurethane lacquer, allowing this to dry before starting work on the roof; further coats can be added later.

## Positioning the frame

You may already have a good idea where you want to install the window but check this exactly at this stage by lifting the frame into position against the roof. Take into account that you will want the control bar within easy reach at the top of the window and perhaps also a view from where you are likely to be sitting.

Once you have worked out the exact position in which you want to fit the window, measure its outside dimensions and carefully transfer these on to the rafters with the help of a spirit level (measurement 'A' in fig. C). Align the base of the marked-out area with the bottom of a course of slates or tiles—this will help to fix the flashing more neatly once the window is in place.

**17** *Replace the tiles or slates down both sides, trimming them to size so that they fit neatly under the edge of the flashing*

**18** *Then replace the top ones, leaving a gap of 60–100mm above the window. Fit a tilting fillet to support a short bottom course*

**19** *Once the roof covering is complete, carefully pick up the sash (taking care not to break the glass) and fit it into the frame*

**20** *Check that the window opens and closes easily. If it sticks, retighten all the screws and make sure the sash is correctly aligned*

Next examine the installation instructions supplied with the window. These specify the clearance required between the frame and the roofing material to ensure a neat fit. Take careful note of the dimensions, marking them onto the roof timbers in a different colour if necessary, so that you know how many tiles or slates to remove (measurement 'B' in fig. C).

Note also that the trimmers which need to be inserted above and below the frame to give it support are not tight against the frame itself: they are set further back to enable the internal window linings to be splayed and so allow a greater spread of light.

First check the thickness of your trimmers and measure and mark this distance above and below the frame position to allow for their width

(measurement 'C' in fig. C). Then allow for the inner splay, using a spirit level to draw horizontal and vertical lines from your new top and bottom marks respectively to the inside of the rafter (measurement 'D' in fig. C). It is at these points that the rafter will be cut and the trimmers nailed into position.

### Cutting an opening

Once you have rechecked that the inside of the roof is correctly marked out, start to remove the roofing materials. How you proceed depends on both the structure of the roof and its covering:

**Tiles and slates:** Start by cutting away any internal roofing felt with a sharp handyman's knife so that you expose the tiles or slates themselves.

Remove these one at a time, starting from the centre and working slowly towards the outside (fig. 4). If they are nailed to the battens, work each tile or slate free with a slate ripper or wedge a trowel under the top edge to break it loose. Continue in this way until you have a space well clear of the area to be occupied by the window.

**Felt roofs:** Using the marks you have made on the inside on the roof as a guide, drill a 20mm diameter hole right through both the wooden decking and the covering felt. Then insert a padsaw and carefully cut around the outside of the marked-out area. When the cut is completed, the inside of the area will drop away and can be lifted clear of the working space.

Once you have removed the roof covering, the next step is to cut away any rafters running across the area to be occupied by the window. But before you do so, make sure that they are supported at top and bottom with timber wedges, placed well away from the area in which you intend to work (see above).

Saw each rafter along the two lines previously marked, trying to keep the cut at the correct angle to the roof. Then prise the freed section away from the roof, taking care not to break or damage any of the battens or roof timbers (fig. 5).

To take the place of the missing rafters fix your trimmers across the top and bottom of the frame. Check carefully that these are correctly aligned with the existing roof timbers and square at each corner before nailing them securely through the uprights and on to the ends of the cut rafter (fig. 6).

With the trimmers set above and below where the frame is to go remove the temporary support and fix a false rafter down one side. Fit this according to the installation instructions so that there is a gap on each side of the frame to allow for the roofing material. Cut the rafter to length, check carefully for alignment and square, then nail it firmly to the trimmers top and bottom (fig. 7).

The window frame should now be placed on the outside of the roof and checked for fit. Do this by sawing down through the centre of the battens or sarking so that you have a slot wide enough to allow the frame to be pushed through sideways (fig. 8). When the frame is on the roof adjust its position exactly—remembering that you will have to replace all the roofing materials around the outside once it is fixed. When you are satisfied that it is

A plywood board, holed and trimmed to size, can be used instead of glass, but needs to be of exterior grade plywood and to be well sealed or painted. This is really only suitable where you are replacing a small window pane.

The appeal of window mounting is that no structural work is involved. Offset against this is the obstructed view, restricted window opening for summer time ventilation and the appearance of the unit.

It takes a little longer to install a wall-mounted fan but the additional effort is usually considered worthwhile. The necessary removal of inner and outer brickwork is not a difficult job for the handyman, especially with the small areas involved here.

The hole should not be made any nearer than two bricks' lengths to a wall edge otherwise structural weakening may occur. In the case of a cavity wall, a liner must be used to seal off the cavity or fumes and moisture will be expelled into it.

**C.** *After you have completed the wiring, fit the face-plate by snapping it into place on the lugs provided on the box*

Extractor fans are also used to give ventilation to internal rooms. Do not be tempted, though, to have the outlet

**D.** *Pull-cord switches hanging from the extractor fan allow you to operate the fan conveniently, and with safety*

from a fan discharge into an unused chimney flue—this is likely to cause condensation problems.

# Cutting a hole in a window

It is generally easier to replace an old pane with a new one ordered from your glass merchant, who will cut the hole for you. However, this may be expensive if the pane is large, and in this case try to cut the hole yourself.

Before doing this, clean the glass on both sides to ensure a clean cut. Then hire a circle glass cutter, which has a sucker base plate and a trammel arm along which the cutter slides. Set the cutter position to give a circle of the required diameter, and draw out the resulting circle on a piece of card so that you can check its size.

You will also need an ordinary glass cutter to criss-cross the cut-out, plus a pair of pliers and a pin hammer.

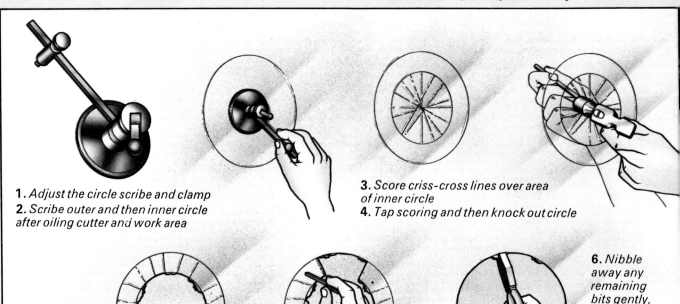

**1.** *Adjust the circle scribe and clamp*
**2.** *Scribe outer and then inner circle after oiling cutter and work area*

**3.** *Score criss-cross lines over area of inner circle*
**4.** *Tap scoring and then knock out circle*

**6.** *Nibble away any remaining bits gently, using a pair of pliers*

**5.** *Score to outer circle then tap and knock out*

# REPAIRING ROOF FLASHINGS

● **What flashings are** ● **The choice in repair materials** ● **Basic repairs** ● **Bending metals** ● **Using flashing tape** ● **Using semi-rigid mineral fibre** ● **Repairing straight flashings, corners and valleys** ● **Mortar flashings**

**A. Above:** *Self-adhesive flashing tape is the simplest to use of all flashing materials and is usually first choice for basic repairs. The tape comes in rolls, together with its own bituminous primer*

External flashing is the term given to the watertight joints between partially separated structures on a house, such as a chimney stack and its surrounding roof area, where a roof butts up against a wall, or where dormer windows and rooflights have been introduced.

Quite simply, it is one of the most vital defences against penetrating damp. Yet, during the regular course of household maintenance and repair, flashing is probably more often neglected than anything else—until, of course, damp patches start to appear on chimney breasts, in the loft or on bedroom and attic ceilings.

In fact, it is a simple process to maintain and repair flashing. Regular checks on its condition should be made from inside the house and are best accomplished in between spells of heavy rainfall. A loft inspection—around the underside of roof valleys and where a chimney stack enters the

roof space—will soon reveal telltale signs of water entry.

Look for water stains on the roof timbers and trace them back to their source. The stains might be yellow, brown or almost black in colour and will appear as streaks along the timber. If the roof covering is slate, the streaks may be white. And if the leak is an old one, fungus might also be present in the form of wet rot.

Searching for leaks can sometimes prove difficult in the confines of a roof space, but you can use a mirror attached to a long pole to help you see under eaves and other difficult areas. Follow up your search by scanning the outside with binoculars.

It is essential that you trace leaks right back to their source. For example, water seen to run down the underside of a valley board does not necessarily mean that the valley liner is at fault. Careful investigation might reveal that the leak is in the

ridge capping and that water is running down a rafter and then on to the valley board.

The flashing on older UK houses is usually made from either lead or zinc, but it is quite common to find other reasonably corrosion-free materials in use—such as duralumin, copper, bituminous felt and semi-rigid mineral fibre (the latter sold in the UK under the trade name Nuralite).

For the do-it-yourself enthusiast, the introduction of self-adhesive flashing has enabled speedy and effective repair work to be carried out. Self-adhesive strip can be purchased in a variety of widths from most hardware stores and consists of heavy duty aluminium foil, sometimes coated with grey lacquer to resemble lead, and backed with a bitumen adhesive. This adhesive surface is protected with siliconized releasing paper which you simply peel off prior to applying the flashing tape itself.

**10** To repair a damaged roof-ridge metal flashing with flashing tape, wire-brush the area and then clean it thoroughly with carborundum paper

**11** Follow by painting on a coat of the special primer. Be sure to extend this well past the actual location of the damage

**12** When the primer is touch dry, cut a suitable length of flashing tape, peel off the backing paper and press it firmly into place

**13** Then iron out the crinkles and air bubbles by rolling over the tape with a hammer handle. Take extra care around the edges as you do this

**14** To cut a length of Nuralite (semi-rigid mineral fibre sheet), score it with a handyman's knife and then snap it against a straightedge

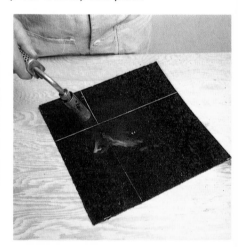

**15** To make an internal corner, cut and mark out the Nuralite as shown then heat the whole area with a blowlamp until it is pliable

**16** Use a wood block soaked with raw linseed oil and the straightedge to bend the softened Nuralite along the first of the folds

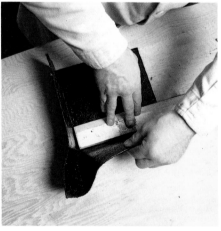

**17** By the time you have finished, the sheet will be hard again—reheat it with the blowlamp before making the second fold

**18** Once the basic creases are there, you can consolidate them with two oiled blocks. Press these hard into the folds and against each other

## Fixing straight flashing

First lever out the old length of flashing and thoroughly rake out the mortar joints to a depth of 25mm.

Next, cut the replacement flashing to length and bend to fit in the manner described above. Remember that you will need to allow for a 19mm turnover strip along its entire length—this will be fed into the mortar joints and must be bent to an angle of 90°.

Wet the mortar joint and insert the turnover into it, wedging with small pieces of the metal you are using.

Now gently hammer the other angled section of the flashing to exactly match the downfall of the roof, taking great care not to accidentally break any tiles or slates. Finally fill the joint with mortar and clean the joint with a piece of rounded stick.

## Replacing mortar flashing

Often, the flashing on a lean-to or garage wall is made up simply from mortar. This has a habit of cracking where it meets the vertical wall, so allowing water to penetrate. Non-hardening mastic can be used to repair small cracks but if the damage is severe, the whole length must be replaced with a proper flashing.

Remove the cement fillet and clean up the exposed brickwork and roof covering. Cut a slot 35mm deep in the abutting vertical wall, at least 75mm above (and parallel to) the adjoining roof. Note that the latter measurement will partially depend upon the location of a convenient mortar joint into which the slot can be cut. The apron—the part of the flashing which overlaps the roof—should be 150mm wide. So the width of the flashing strip should be 260–300mm.

**19** *When you get to the corner, make the flap face outwards and press it together with the blocks. Add more heat if the sheet is too rigid*

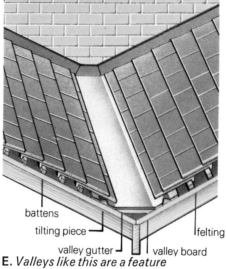

**E.** *Valleys like this are a feature of older properties. The metal linings are notoriously prone to deterioration and should be patched with flashing tape or semi-rigid asbestos*

battens
tilting piece
valley gutter
valley board
felting

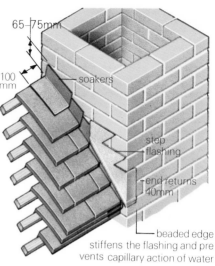

65–75mm
100 mm
soakers
step flashing
end returns 40mm
beaded edge stiffens the flashing and prevents capillary action of water

**F.** *The stepped soakers which form part of the flashings at chimneys and roof verges were traditionally cut from sheet metal; today you can buy them preformed in semi-rigid fibre*

The flashing is secured by forcing the 35mm turnover into the slot in the wall and wedging it in place with small, rolled pieces of the same metal. This slot is then filled with a 1:4 mortar mix.

If you are using lead, you will need to provide extra support with additional strips of metal called *tingles*. These are nailed into the rafters between the slates or tiles. Then, after the flashing is laid, they are bent over the front edge of the apron to stop it sliding down the roof.

## Valley linings

Valley linings (fig. E) are a common feature of older properties—the very houses where damage due to ageing is likely to occur.

Small cracks and rents can be treated in much the same way as described for flashing, using either patches made up from self-adhesive flashing or a foil and mastic combination. Here, though, it is vital that the whole valley is treated with liquid bituminous proofing or a suitable liquid plastic coating.

Severe damage will inevitably mean total replacement and, as you will be removing a substantial number of tiles either side of the valley, ensure that you can quickly protect the exposed area from rain. Tarpaulin or heavy duty reinforced plastic sheet is ideal. You can replace the old lining with zinc or lead sheet, or even roofing felt, but probably the simplest cure is to use self-adhesive strip.

For the more traditional approach, you must first remove all the tiles

covering both sides of the valley edge. Pull up the old lining and carefully lower it down to ground level. And while you are there, take the opportunity to check the state of the timber underlining; it is worthwhile treating it at this stage with a coat of preservative.

When you cut the new length of zinc or lead allow an overlap of about 50mm at the eaves. Place the new sheet over the underlining and work it into the shape of the valley, securing with galvanized nails.

Should you need to use more than one sheet, allow plenty of overlap between adjoining sheets to prevent water returning between them. You must also provide for a 75mm turning where the sheet meets the junction between wall and roof (fig. E).

Finish by securing the sheet to the battens on both sides working up from the eaves, and replacing the tiles in reverse number order. Use self-adhesive flashing along the length of the roof/wall junction to ensure effective waterproofing.

## Flashing on a corner

Traditionally done with metal, flashing on a corner can be extremely difficult for the home handyman. The way to do it depends on the metal being used, but all methods demand a range of specialized tools and practical skills which are generally best left to a specialist.

One convenient material available for the do-it-yourselfer in the UK is semi-rigid mineral fibre sheet called Nuralite. This material is light in

**20** Finish off the corner shaping using a wooden former made from two offcuts of blockboard

**21** To make an external corner, mark a length as shown with one longitudinal line and five centre lines to indicate the four centre folds

**22** Then, using the same heating-forming-heating process, fold the centre folds over one another to shorten the length by two folds

weight, waterproof and resistant to both abrasion and corrosion. It is easy to cut and, when heated with a blowtorch, can be bent and shaped. Nuralite also can be used as a roof covering and for making straight flashings in preference to lead or zinc figs B, D, F and 14 to 24).

**Cutting:** Straight cuts can be made by scoring deeply with a sharp knife and then breaking off the piece over the edge of a workbench or scaffold plank. Cut special shapes or irregular sections with a pair of tin-snips.

**Bending:** Use a crayon, pencil, or chalk line to mark the position of the bend. Place the line squarely over the edge of your bench and hold the sheet in position with a wooden batten cramped over the top.

Apply a blowtorch flame up and down the length of the area to be bent until the sheet begins to sweat and gradually bend of its own accord. As it does so, help form the shape slowly and firmly using a wooden block until you achieve the required angle. Both the block and the batten must be well sanded and kept lubricated with linseed oil or candlewax to prevent them sticking to the hot Nuralite.

For a bend of 90° turn over the sheet, align the angle point with the edge of the bench, reheat the sheet and press down the upstand with the wooden block until you achieve the right angle.

**Joining:** There are two methods used for joining this type of material—*delaminating* and *lap jointing*.

To delaminate Nuralite, heat the edge of one sheet, insert a knife blade into it and turn back about 25mm of the top layer of Nuralite. Next, melt

**23** The folded length should now look like this. As before, consolidate the folds with oiled blocks and reheat if necessary

some bitumen No 1 welding block—available from larger builders' merchants—on to the inner surfaces and smooth it out using a paintscraper and heat from a blowtorch. Place the adjoining sheet between the two delaminated sections of the first and then heat them again with your blowtorch. Finally, consolidate the edges with a sealing or soldering iron.

For a lapped joint, both the surfaces to be joined must be well coated with No 3 bitumen compound (again available in block form). When working over small areas, heat the compound with a blowtorch and apply it directly to the sheets with a paint scraper. On larger surfaces, heat the bitumen block in a pot and then apply it with a suitable brush.

Heat the area to be coated and

**24** Do the remaining corner shaping on the blockboard former, heating at intervals so that the centre folds splay out as shown

spread No 3 compound on both mating surfaces to a minimum width of 75mm. Bring the two together, apply more heat and flatten the entire area of the joint with a heated trowel.

### Safety

When working at or above roof level always give thought to the safety of yourself and others. Use recognized scaffolding which is properly secured at ground level. Never leave tools or other heavy items unattended on the roof—they could slide off and hit someone. Try, whenever possible to work in company with someone else or at least make sure that help is close at hand if you need it.

# UNDERSTANDING ELECTRICITY

**Electric current explained ● Units of electrical measurement ● Loop, radial and ring-main circuits ● Earthing ● Fuses and circuit breakers ● Mending fuses ● Wiring a plug**

**Above:** *Electricity is very much taken for granted in homes today, because it is available at the flick of a switch*

Electricity in the home is something which we all take for granted—and would be lost without. Yet electricity is also highly dangerous if it is not treated with the respect it deserves. For the do-it-yourself enthusiast, this means having a sound knowledge of the way in which domestic installations work before tackling any electrical job with confidence.

## Electricity and the law
In the UK, regulations covering wiring are compiled by the Institute of Electrical Engineers. Anyone may do their own wiring, but it is very sensible to follow the IEE regulations. These require that all electrical installations be tested on completion by the relevant electricity supply board.

## Electrical measures
An electric current consists of a flow of minute particles called electrons. This flow can be likened to the flow of water from a tap connected by a pipe to a storage tank.

For water to flow when the tap is opened, the tank must be at a higher level than the tap. And the greater the height of the tank, the higher the pressure of the water that comes out of the tap. So water at high pressure has a greater rate of flow, or current, than water at low pressure.

The *voltage* in an electrical circuit corresponds with the *pressure* of the water in the pipe. The *rate* of flow of an electric current is measured in *amperes* and is equivalent to the flow of water along the pipe—that is, how much comes out at any given time.

Electrical power is measured in *watts*. This term applies to the electrical equipment itself and is a measurement of the rate at which it uses electricity. An average electric light bulb uses only about 100 watts, whereas a powerful electric heater might use 3,000 watts (3 kilowatts). The relationship between amps, volts and watts is expressed in the formula:

$$\frac{\text{Watts}}{\text{Volts}} = \text{Amps}$$

This formula is useful for determining both the correct size of cable to use for an appliance and, in British systems, the correct size of cartridge fuse inserted in its plug.

## Domestic installations
The comparison between the flow of water in a pipe and an electric current in a wire is not exact: electricity requires a closed loop—a circuit—in order to work.

Electricity comes into the home from a local transformer through an armoured service cable or via overhead wires. The service cable is connected to a fuse unit—called the company fuse—which is sealed by the electricity board or company. From here, power flows along the live supply wire and through the meter to the consumer unit—a

> **WARNING**
> In Australia and New Zealand, work on electrical installations must be approved by the supply authority and supervised by a licensed electrician.

comes faulty, only the fuse in its own plug—and not the main fuse for the whole circuit—will 'blow'.

## Modern radials

Many modern wiring installations use a variation of the loop-in system already described for lighting circuits. Here the circuit cable runs from socket to socket, originating at the consumer unit and terminating at the last socket (see D). Modern radial circuits of this type may be wired up in two different ways depending on the floor area of the rooms they are serving—see Electrician 2, pages 7-10—but in each case the circuit may serve an unlimited number of sockets. Furthermore, spurs may be taken off the circuit to serve isolated sockets, as for ring-main extensions.

Modern radial circuits use the same 13-amp rectangular pin type of plug and socket as a ring-main. This means that, unlike old radial circuits, there are two levels of fuse protection—within the appliance plug itself, and also at the main consumer unit.

## Earthing

Should a live wire come into contact with the metal casing of an appliance, anyone who touches the appliance is liable to receive a severe electric shock. For this reason, domestic appliances—apart from ones that are double insulated—have an earth wire connected to their outer casings and linked to the house earthing point.

This is so that, if a live wire makes contact with the casing, the electricity will follow the path of least resistance to earth; in other words, it will flow through the earth wire instead of the person's body. At the same time, a live wire coming into contact with earthed metalwork will result in a large current flow that also will blow the circuit or plug fuse.

The electricity flows from the live wire in this way because it is trying to reach the neutral—which is connected to earth back at the electricity board transformer. This system has been found to be the safest way of disposing of unwanted current.

## Fuses

A fuse is a deliberately weak link in the wiring, thinner than the wires on either side. If an overload occurs, the fuse wire melts and cuts off the current before the heat from the overload can damage equipment or cause a fire.

Fuses should always be of the nearest available size above the amperage of the appliance or circuit that they protect. Most electrical appliances have their wattage marked on a small plate fixed to the back or base of the unit. So, for an appliance connected to a ring-main, you can use the formula above to find the amp rating and hence the correct fuse to go in the appliance's plug.

For example, say an electric fire has a rating of 3 kilowatts and the voltage of the mains is 240 volts. The current taken by the fire is found by dividing the watts—3,000—by the volts—240—which gives a result of 12.5 amps. Therefore, the fire should be protected with a 13-amp fuse, the nearest higher size available.

In Britain, it is recommended practice to use 3-amp cartridge fuses, colour coded red, for all appliances rated up to 720 watts, and 13-amp fuses, colour coded brown, for everything else up to a maximum rating of 3 kilowatts—including TV sets, which take a high start-up current even though they are rated at below 720 watts, and so may blow a 3-amp fuse.

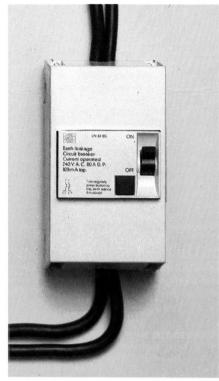

**Above:** A residual current device (RCD) provides an additional level of safety by cutting the supply when it detects an earth current leak

## Residual current devices

Many modern wiring systems incorporate an additional safety measure called a residual current device (RCD)—formerly known as an earth leakage circuit breaker (ELCB). This detects current leaking to earth as a result of an electrical fault and shuts off the current in a fraction of a second if one occurs. This device may be fitted in a modern consumer unit (see page 103) or in a separate enclosure (as above).

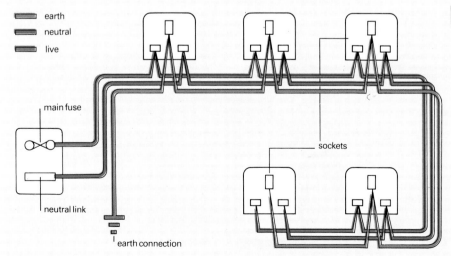

earth
neutral
live

main fuse

neutral link

earth connection

sockets

# Modern radial circuit

*F. A modern radial circuit is wired like a loop-in lighting circuit, with the circuit cable running outwards from the consumer unit to each socket in turn, and terminating at the last socket on the circuit. It's a useful alternative to the ring main for adding circuits to extensions and conversions, or for reaching remote parts of the house where running a ring-main out and back would waste cable unnecessarily. The actual connections are made in exactly the same way as for a ring-main, and spurs may be taken off the circuit if required*

# Mend a fuse

There are three main types of circuit fuse: wire fuses, cartridge fuses and circuit breakers. It is important to know which type you have and to keep a supply of spare fuse wire or cartridges. Circuit breakers need no spares as they are switches which automatically shut off if the circuit is overloaded at any time.

Most fuse boxes are covered by a plate which either clips on or screws into place. **Always turn off the mains switch before removing the plate or touching any fuse.**

With the plate removed you will see a row of fuse holders made of porcelain or moulded plastic (fig. G). Some are colour coded on the base: white for 5 amp lighting circuits, blue for 15 amp heating circuits, red for 30 amp power socket circuits and green for 45 amp cooker circuits. Alternatively, the amperage may be stamped on the front of the holder.

As a further guide it is a good idea to mark the fuse holders with the purpose of the circuit they protect—'1st floor sockets', 'Ground floor lights' and so on.

Take out the first fuse—the holders simply pull out and clip back into place—then replace the cover and turn the mains switch back on.

Check each circuit until you find the one that has stopped working. Turn off the mains again, remove the cover and mark the fuse holder accordingly. Afterwards, clip it back into place and repeat the operation for the other fuses in the box.

When a fuse blows, the first thing to do is to discover the cause and rectify it. If you suspect that the failure is due to a faulty appliance, unplug it and do not use it again until it has been mended.

Sometimes fuses blow for no obvious reason. It may be that the fuse has just worn out in which case when it is replaced, the current will flow as before. But if a fuse keeps blowing each time it is replaced, there may well be a serious fault and you should contact an electrician.

Once the fault that caused the fuse to blow has been put right, locate the blown fuse. On *bridge wire* fuse holders (fig. G), the fuse wire is held in position by a screw at either end. The wire runs over the surface of the holder, so a broken fuse can be clearly seen. In *protected wire* fuse holders, the wire runs through a tube inside the holder. To check it, gently try to prise the wire out of the tube with a small screwdriver. If the fuse is blown, half of the wire will come away.

To mend a wire fuse, loosen the screws and discard the broken wire.

Replacement fuse wire is sold ready for use, mounted on a card. Use wire-cutters to cut a new length of wire of the correct amperage rating. Wrap the ends of the wire around the screws in a clockwise direction so that when you retighten the screws the wire is not dislodged. Finally, replace the holder and fuse box cover and switch the power back on.

In cartridge fuses, the wire is encased in the cartridge and can only be checked, at this stage, by replacement. Unclip the old cartridge and fit a replacement of the same amperage rating as the original.

When a circuit breaker shuts off, locate the fault that has caused it to do so, then reset the switch or button on the affected circuit.

When mending fuses, on no account be tempted to use a fuse of too high an amperage rating; you will be putting your entire electrical system—and possibly your life—at risk.

All the equipment you need for mending fuses—screwdriver, wire cutters and pliers—should be electrically insulated for maximum protection from electric shock.

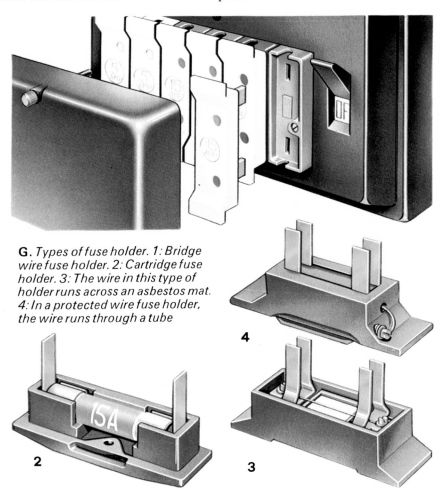

**G.** *Types of fuse holder. 1: Bridge wire fuse holder. 2: Cartridge fuse holder. 3: The wire in this type of holder runs across an asbestos mat. 4: In a protected wire fuse holder, the wire runs through a tube*

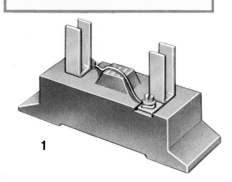

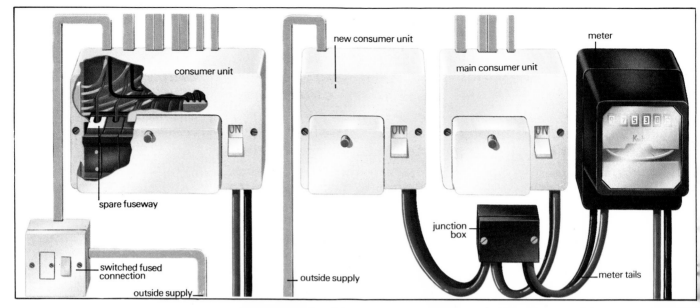

new consumer unit

consumer unit

main consumer unit

meter

spare fuseway

junction box

switched fused connection

outside supply

outside supply

meter tails

**B.** *Outdoor circuits need providing with special protection to prevent any possibility of electric shocks. So as well as a fuse or MCB (miniature circuit breaker) fit into the circuit a high-sensitivity residual current device or RCD (sometimes called a residual current circuit breaker, or RCCB). The switched fused connector (shown above) can carry the RCD (not shown). If you have a spare fuseway, add an extra consumer unit which the electricity board will connect via a junction box to their meter.*

To connect the armoured cables to the house and outbuilding circuits you will need special compression joints for connection to a steel junction box.
**Size of cable:** For a 20 amp supply over a distance greater than 20m, use 4mm² cable. You can also use 4mm² cable for 30 amp runs of less than 20m, but on longer runs you will need 6mm² cable to prevent excessive voltage drop.

**Overhead cable installation**
Drill a hole for the cable through an outside wall, so that the cable will lie beneath the upstairs floorboards. If that position does not give you enough height, go into the roof space and drill a hole through the wall above ceiling level or through the fascia board or soffit at the eaves.

Next feed the required length of cable through the hole and let it drop to the ground while you erect the post at the outbuilding end. Seal the hole with a non-hardening mastic. Mark off the end of the post which will be buried and then drill holes to take the

**1** *When running a cable along an outside wall, use armoured cable of the correct size for its length and then fasten it with stout clips*

**2** *Drill and plug holes in the brickwork for the clips and secure them with wood screws. Do not drill into mortar as this may cause it to crumble*

**3** *Drill through house walls below the DPC, making sure you do not damage services inside the house. Use a long masonry bit for cavity walls*

**4** *Allow enough length of cable for connection inside the house before feeding it through the wall and sealing the hole with non-hardening mastic*

expanding wall bolts.

Lower the post, drill the holes in the wall, and then screw an eye-bolt securely into the top of the post. Attach one end of the support wire to this, cut it to the correct length and then securely fix a wire tensioner to the other end.

The support wire must be bonded to earth for safety reasons. Connect one end of a length of 2.5mm² green and yellow PVC insulated cable to the eye-bolt and clip this to the post using cable clips. Allow enough length for the cable to be attached to the switched fused connection unit.

Next run the power cable from the house to the outbuilding and lay it alongside the support wire. Allow enough extra length to reach the inside of the building from the top of the post and then clip it to the support wire using stout cable ties every 1m or so. Raise the post again, fit it into its hole and bolt it to the wall. Fill in the hole

and compact the earth around the post as hard as you can by stamping on it.

Returning to the house, get up on a ladder and drill and plug a hole in the wall or the eaves for another eye-bolt as close as possible to the cable entry point. Screw in the eye and then pull the free end of the cable support wire up to it. Fix the wire securely and take up the slack with the tensioning device. Inside the house take up the slack on the cable and either run the wire directly back to the consumer unit or cut it off close to the entry point and leave about 3m inside the house for connection.

## Underground cables
Decide first where the cable will enter the house—you will have to drill a hole for the cable through one of the walls above the DPC or through a corner of an air brick. If you cannot do this without going through

the wall above the floorboards, or if you have a solid floor, choose a room where the sight of exposed cable does not matter too much—a laundry room is ideal.

Once you have finalized the route of the trench, mark it out with string and pegs and start digging. The trench should be 500mm deep and about 300mm wide. When you have finished, remove any flints or sharp stones from the base and cover it with a 50mm layer of fine sand or sifted soil to act as a cushion.

Armoured cable can be laid directly into the trench, but if you are using PVC sheathed cable and conduit assemble the conduit first to make sure it fits before dismantling it again and threading the cable through. Allow about 1m of cable inside each building for connection.

Secure the conduit or cable to the walls with saddle fasteners and lay slabs of concrete over the cable in the trench to protect it from spades and forks at a later date. Fill in the trench compacting the earth as you do so.

### Outside walls
Where the cable can be run along the outside wall of the house or along a garden wall, use the same cable types as for underground installations. Pass the cable through the house wall in the same way as for underground or overhead installations, depending on how high off the ground you intend to route it. Secure the cable to the walls using saddle fasteners.

### Supply and connections
Once you have installed the outside cables, you can lay the supply cables inside the house. If you have a spare fuseway inside the consumer unit, use this for the supply to the outbuilding. If not, ask the electricity board to cut off the power and connect a supply from the meter to a new consumer unit once you have completed the rest of the installation.

Start by screwing a fixed appliance outlet or new consumer unit to the wall next to the consumer unit—this will allow you to isolate the entire cable and outbuilding circuit without having to fiddle with the fuses in the unit (fig. B).

Connect to the outlet a length of twin and earth cable of the same cross-sectional area as the cable outside. Run the outer end of the cable to the consumer unit and leave it there. Now run more of the same cable from the switched fuse connection unit to the outside cable entry point—follow normal wiring practice in routing and fixing it.

If the outside cable is twin and earth PVC sheathed, connect the two using a junction box screwed to the inside wall, to a floor joist below the floorboards, or to a ceiling joist in the roof space. If the outside

**5** Remove any turf on the route of an underground cable before digging a trench 500mm deep and about 300mm wide in which to bury it

**6** Unroll the cable into the trench, making sure that it is not kinked. For a garden socket, allow 1m of cable at the end of the trench for connection

**7** Cover the cable with fine sand or soil before laying slabs of concrete or concrete cable tiles to protect it from garden spades and forks

**8** Prepare Pyrotenax for connection by stripping off the outer PVC sheathing for about 150mm and slipping the rubber boot over the end

cable is MICS or armoured, cut it off inside the house at a suitable mounting point for a junction box. Screw a steel knockout switch box directly to the inside wall or a joist at this point and remove a knockout on two opposite sides.

Prepare the outside cable by stripping off about 150mm of the outer PVC and armoured sheathing to expose the wires. The compression fittings which join the cable to the switch box are exactly the same as those for copper pipe and are fitted in the same way. Slip the capnut over the PVC sheathing and then fit and tighten the threaded gland. Insert the fitting into one of the holes in the box and secure it with a back nut. Fit a PVC grommet over the other hole in the box, slip the PVC sheathed cable through and connect the two cables using a three-way terminal block. Use a blanking plate to seal the box.

Repeat the connection procedure at the outbuilding end then run twin and earth cable of the correct cross-sectional area to a switched fused connection unit mounted on the wall near the door. From here, run the cable to the lights, switches, and socket outlets in the building.

## Outside lighting

Outside lighting takes many forms, ranging from floodlights mounted on the house walls, or concealed in the garden, to courtesy lights mounted at the end of the drive on the gate posts. A wide range of weatherproof lights is available, most of which operate on mains voltage. Some – taking bulbs similar to car headlamp units – operate at a lower voltage and require a transformer.

Power supplies to outside lights are run

**9** *Slip the compression fittings over the end of the exposed copper sheathing and slide them well down the cable out of the way*

**10** *Now strip back about 70mm of the copper sheathing. As you do this the mineral insulation will crumble away to expose the cable cores*

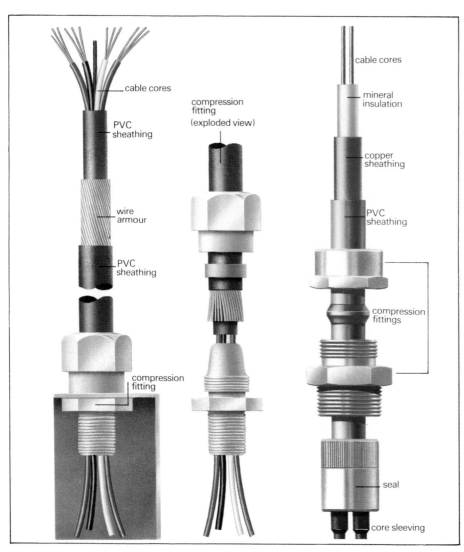

cable cores

compression fitting (exploded view)

PVC sheathing

wire armour

PVC sheathing

compression fitting

cable cores

mineral insulation

copper sheathing

PVC sheathing

compression fittings

seal

core sleeving

**11** *Screw the pot on to the exposed copper sheathing using a pair of pliers – making sure that it goes on absolutely straight*

**C.** *The two main types of armoured cable: PVC sheathed wire-armoured cable (left and centre) shown with its compression fittings exploded and fitted* *to a switch box. Pyrotenax armoured cable (right) is shown with its slightly different compression fittings and watertight seals in place*

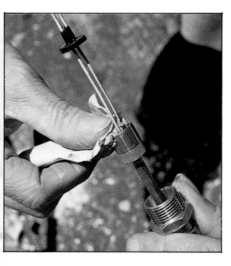

**12** *Slip the watertight seal over the ends of the cores and then press sealing compound firmly into the pot to separate them*

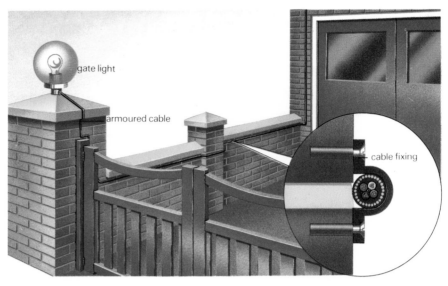

**13** *Press the seal down hard to compress the compound and then slip sleeving over the cores, leaving about 20mm exposed for connection*

**14** *Mark one of the cores with a piece of red tape to identify it as the live wire and use a meter or test bulb to identify the other end*

**15** *Attach Pyrotenax to a switch or junction box by slipping the compression gland into a knockout hole and securing it with a back nut*

in exactly the same way – and using the same materials – as the supply to an outbuilding. The only exception is where a light is fixed directly to the outside wall of the house: here you can supply the unit through a hole drilled in the wall with the switch inside the house.

Gate lights can be supplied with either an underground or a wall-mounted cable, MICS and armoured cable being run directly to the light fitting itself. If you wish to install an outside switch as well, use a weatherproof lockable key switch to prevent tampering by vandals and children. These are fitted and connected in exactly the same way as their domestic counterparts indoors.

Transformers should ideally be located inside the house or an outbuilding but many are weatherproof and can be located discreetly in the garden. Make sure, however, that all the cable entry points are protected by weatherproof seals.

**D. Above**: *An outside gate light with a wall-mounted power supply. This kind of supply can be used for other types of light and also for garden sockets*

**Fairy lights:** There are a number of units ideal for fairy lights. These have two steel pins projecting from the lampholder which are protected by a weatherproof screw-on cover and are called Festoon lampholders (fig. E).

To connect the lampholders run a twin and earth 4mm² seven-strand cable from a 13 amp socket in the house or the garden (see below) and lay it out on a lawn or similar flat surface. Unscrew the cover on the pins, press the cable on to them so that one pin pierces each core, and screw the cap firmly back in place.

Use a maximum of 10 lampholders per circuit with a bulb rating of 40 watts. The last lampholder on the circuit should conceal the cut end of the cable.

When you hang the lights – whether in a tree or from a support wire slung between two poles, trees or buildings – make sure that the cables are not under tension and that the bulbs cannot get blown against branches or walls; if this happens, the bulb may break and expose the filaments which could be dangerous in wet weather.

Once you have made up a set of fairy lights in this way, do not remove any of the lampholders or you will expose holes in the wire which, in wet weather, could cause a short circuit.

## Garden socket outlets

Because so many garden tools are now electrically powered, a socket outlet in the garden can be very useful. And if your garden is quite small you may be able to fit the socket on the outside wall of the house or outbuilding.

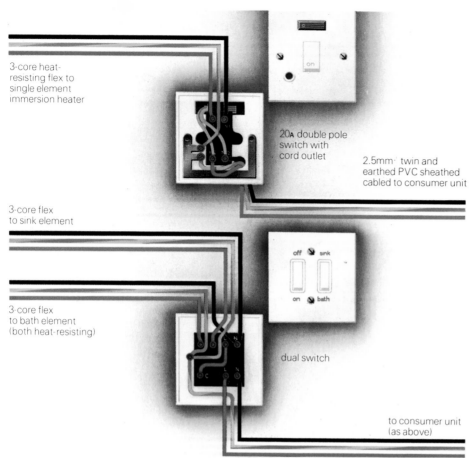

3-core heat-
resisting flex to
single element
immersion heater

20A double pole
switch with
cord outlet

2.5mm· twin and
earthed PVC sheathed
cabled to consumer unit

3-core flex
to sink element

off ⚑ sink

on ⚑ bath

3-core flex
to bath element
(both heat-resisting)

dual switch

to consumer unit
(as above)

**A. Left:** *A 20A double-pole switch used in an immersion heater circuit. Switched outlets must be positioned outside a bathroom*
**Below left:** *A special dual switch used in a twin element immersion heater circuit*

Because of this, it is only safe to supply something as powerful as an immersion heater from a ring circuit spur if the circuit is lightly loaded—such as one supplying the upstairs part of the house only.

But for other, less demanding, appliances, taking the supply from a ring circuit spur is the ideal solution as long as the number of unfused spurs from the circuit does not exceed the number of socket outlets already present.

Where an appliance is supplied from a ring circuit spur, it is essential that a fuse—the equivalent of the fuse in a 13 amp plug—be inserted somewhere in the spur circuit. Without this, the only protection the circuit would have is the 30 amp fuse in the consumer unit which requires up to 60 amps to blow it if it's the rewirable type.

### Direct from the consumer unit

If you have a spare fuseway in your consumer unit, taking an exclusive circuit from here is usually a simple job—and in the case of an immersion heater, almost essential.

Where there are no spare fuseways, you can either replace the consumer unit with one containing more fuseways—a rather expensive solution—or install a *switchfuse* unit which is, in effect, a small consumer unit containing one or two fuses.

### Ring circuit spurs

Though ring circuit spurs can be used to supply any of the above mentioned appliances, you must be careful not to overload the ring circuit. For example, while an extractor fan takes about 40 watts and a heat/light unit about 700 watts, an immersion heater takes 3000 watts and is better run on a separate radial circuit.

In the UK, the maximum load capacity of a ring circuit is 7200 watts; but for safety reasons it is wise not to exceed a loading of 6500 watts. So if you supply an immersion heater—which is classed as a continuous load—from a ring circuit, you immediately take up half the recommended loading.

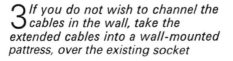

2 *Disconnect the socket and extend the cables using connector blocks Use 2.5mm² twin core and earth, PVC sheathed cable*

3 *If you do not wish to channel the cables in the wall, take the extended cables into a wall-mounted pattress, over the existing socket*

4 *Take a switched fused connection unit, and nibble away an opening in the rear of the pattress to run the cable from the socket outlet*

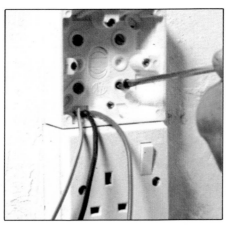

5 *Connect the extended cables up to the socket back, then connect another set of cables to the socket and run them up to the connector*

6 *Mark the position of the pattress on the wall, directly above the socket, then drill the holes, plug the wall and fix the pattress in place*

7 *Strip about 9mm of insulation off each of the cables and then connect them up to the appropriate terminals on the connection unit*

## Fixed outlets

As mentioned above, you have a choice of three types of fixed outlet.

**Fused connection unit:** This is quite simply a terminal box and fuse carrier containing a small cartridge fuse. It is housed in a square, one-gang cover plate (faceplate) for mounting in a standard, one-gang plastics or metal box. The fuses are identical to those fitted in 13 amp fused plugs.

In the UK, they are stamped BS.1362 and the 13 amp is brown, the 10 amp black, the 5 amp black, the 3 amp red and the 2 amp black. When buying these fuses, take great care to purchase the right ones: slightly smaller ones are available which are marked BS.646, and are intended for use in dimmer switches, shaver socket outlets and the like, not in fused connection units.

Fused connection units come in two forms—switched and non-switched—and have a flex outlet attached and/or a neon indicator.

**Double-pole switch:** This is a rocker switch on a standard, square one-gang faceplate for mounting in a standard 1-gang plastic or metal box. Used as the mains outlet for a fixed appliance, it has a 20 amp current rating.

Like fused units, double-pole switches come in a variety of styles—

with and without a neon indicator and with and without a flex outlet—but because they contain no fuses, you must fit one of the appropriate current rating somewhere in the circuit.

**Flex outlet unit:** Also known as a cord outlet, this is a square, one-gang standard faceplate with a hole in the centre through which a circular, sheathed flex can pass. At the back of the plate is a three-way terminal block and a flex, or cord, clamp. The function of the unit is to connect the flex which feeds the appliance to the fixed circuit wiring. In fact it is used in much the same way as a ceiling rose in a lighting circuit.

A flex outlet is generally used as the mains outlet to a fixed appliance where no other outlet may be used, such as in a bathroom where a low-mounted wall heater needs to be controlled by a remote, cord-operated, ceiling switch.

## Connecting a fixed spur

Where a ring circuit spur is to supply a fixed appliance, the spur cable should be connected to the ring main at a convenient point. Typically this will be either at the terminals of an existing ring socket outlet, or at a 30 amp three-terminal joint box inserted into the ring cable at a con-

venient place, such as under the floorboards.

For many appliances—such as wall heaters, waste disposers and central heating electrics—the necessary fuse for the spur can be that in the fused connection unit fixed near the appliance and connected to it by flexible cord or cable.

The spur cable from the point where it joins the ring circuit to the fused connection unit must be 2.5mm². The size of the flex from the connection unit will be smaller and must be suited to the connection unit fuse—itself determined by the type of appliance.

Where the outlet unit is to be a double-pole switch or a flex outlet, the necessary fuse should be situated away from the appliance. The best position is at, or near, the point where the spur cable is connected to the ring cable and will take the form of a non-switched, fused connection unit. This can be fixed next to the ring socket outlet to which the spur is connected.

Where the spur is supplied from a joint box, you run a 2.5mm² cable from the joint box to the non-switched

**B. Below:** *Connect up a 2.5mm² spur from a ring circuit cable by cutting in a three-terminal junction box*

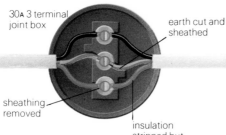

30A 3 terminal joint box

earth cut and sheathed

ring cable

sheathing removed

insulation stripped but wire not cut

ring cable

spur cable

has a removable 'plug' to which the flex is connected and contains a fuse of either 3 amp or 1 amp rating. Removing the 'plug' isolates the fan from the mains electricity.

When a fan is supplied from a lighting circuit, no fuse is needed but a clock connector is still the best accessory for connecting the fan flex to the fixed circuit wiring. Where the extractor fan does not contain a cord-operated switch, or where a reversing facility is needed, a control switch can be fixed at a lower level and the circuit wiring run to the controller first.

## Waste disposer
A waste disposer requires a switched fused connection unit, ideally supplied from a ring circuit spur. With many models of waste disposer the control

**F. Below:** *The various circuits for fixed appliances in the kitchen. All the appliances require a fused spur. Note how the extractor fan circuit on the left is fused, properly, before the control unit. (Left to right) The circuits are for an extractor fan, a water heater, a waste disposal unit, and a central heating boiler. In all cases you must use a 2.5mm² cable from the ring circuit*

unit—which sometimes includes a reversing control—is mounted on the disposer body. The flex from the fused connection unit should run direct to this controller and be connected to the mains terminals. Where the controller is a separate unit, it can be mounted next to the fused connection unit.

As this is a low-level mains outlet, it is best—where possible—to run the spur cable up from below the kitchen floor where it can be connected to a 30 amp joint box inserted into the ring cable. If you have a solid floor, run the spur from a socket outlet situated above the work surfaces.

## Central heating outlet
The mains outlet for a central heating pump and controls usually presents the same problems as a waste disposer outlet as this, too, is fixed at a low level. It is best located on the wall as near as possible to the pump or controller mains terminals. The outlet should be a switched fused connection unit with a flex outlet. Alternatively, you could use a 13 amp socket outlet, though there is always the chance that the plug will be accidentally withdrawn to enable another appliance to be used, and not be replaced immediately.

The sheathed flexible cord should be

of the heat-resisting type. With some installations, cable—rather than flex—is used for the connection. If so, the fused connection unit should not have a flex outlet. Although not essential, it is useful to have a plate with a neon indicator.

Before wiring the circuit and fixing the mains outlet, you should consult the manufacturer's instructions provided with the boiler, pump and controls: the electrical requirements differ between different installations.

## Kitchen electrical appliances
Most electrical appliances used in the kitchen are completely portable and are plugged into socket outlets, but for those which are fixed, a supply taken from a switched fused connection unit is most convenient. Washing machines, dishwashers, freezers and refrigerators with a loading of not more than 3000 watts can all be supplied from 13 amp mains outlets. Conventional electric cookers have much higher loadings and require 30 or 45 amp circuits. This will be covered later in the course.

The fused connection units for fixed appliances can either be supplied from ring circuit spurs or wired into the ring cable of the circuit as they are installed.

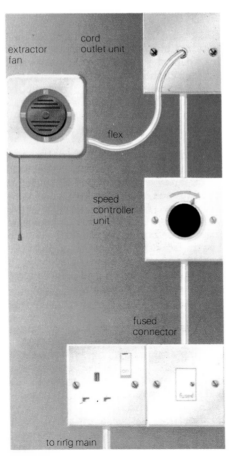
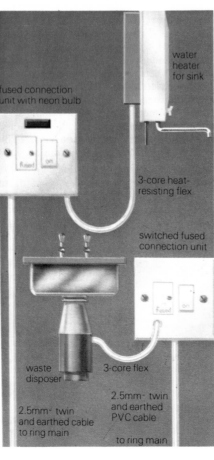
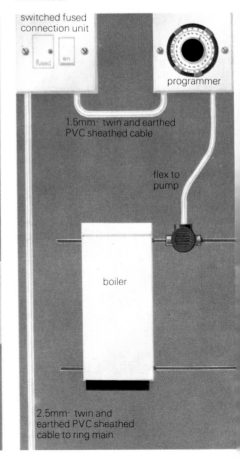

# INSTALLING A PORCH LIGHT

A porch light does more than light the way to your front door: it also acts as a powerful deterrent to prowlers. Fitting one as an extension to your house lighting is a simple job.

A porch light is good way to brighten up your home—it says 'welcome' to the guests you want, and it helps deter the prowlers you'd rather not have around. And by lighting the way to your front door, it can help prevent accidents on dark nights.

### Types of fitting
Most 'porch' lights are not actually fitted inside a porch—if the porch is fully enclosed and weatherproof you could fit an ordinary light fitting in it—but are usually fitted just outside the front or back door, often on the house wall. They can also be hung from the roof of open porch canopies.

Although there are hundreds of different porch lights on the market, they fall into about half a dozen broad categories. The basic types are:
**carriage lanterns**—reproductions of old-fashioned coach lights, designed for wall mounting;
**hanging lanterns**—similar in style to carriage lanterns, but designed to be hung from the ceiling;
**globe lights**—modern versions of the old carriage lantern, with a clear or opaque globe surrounding the bulb;
**bulkhead light**—functional ship-style light with a flush base and toughened glass or plastic cover, often with a wire grille for extra protection;

**Left:** *A porch light illuminates the way to your front door, providing a warm welcome for guests, and also helps to deter unwelcome prowlers*

**brick light**—similar to a bulkhead light, but with a plain rectangular or circular diffuser;
**spotlight**—special exterior types fitted with PAR (parabolic aluminised reflector) bulbs.

Whichever type you choose, it is vital that the lamp is designed for exterior use and is marked as such. Check carefully before you buy.

### Planning the wiring
The wiring for the new light circuit must be run in 1.0mm² two-core and earth cable, and if it will be exposed on the outside wall of the house instead of running straight through the wall into the back of the fitting, it must be protected by high-impact plastic conduit sealed at the ends. Cable of this size must be protected by a 5-amp circuit fuse, so if you borrow power from a ring circuit you must do so via a fused connection unit containing a 5-amp fuse to provide the necessary sub-circuit protection (see Finding a power source).

In most cases, the best position for a porch light switch is just inside the hall door. However, a switch outside the house is also useful, allowing you to switch the light on when you come home and to find your front door key easily. If you use an outside switch, it must be a splashproof type. You can, of course, have both indoor and outdoor switches, wired up like those controlling your hall and landing lights indoors.

### Finding a power source
The first job is to find an existing circuit into which you can tap to provide power for the new light (note that you can do this only for a light on the outside of the house wall; a remote light or lights must have its own independent circuit running from the consumer unit). You can tap into either a light circuit or a power circuit (as the illustrations overleaf explain), and the best place to look for a convenient connection point is usually underneath the upstairs floorboards, close to the projected position of the outside light.

The simplest way of making the connection is by inserting a four-terminal junction box into the existing lighting circuit cable (fig. A), and then

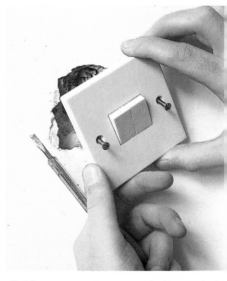

**6** *If you are running your spur from a lighting or power circuit cable, isolate it and connect in a three-terminal junction box*

**7** *Where cable runs have to cross joists, drill 12mm diameter holes through the joist centres. Secure runs parallel to joists with cable clips*

**8** *If you are using the existing switch drop to the hall light position, replace the old one-gang switch with a two-gang type*

through the wall directly behind the fitting baseplate, so it's completely concealed from the outside. Drill a 10mm (⅜in) diameter hole through the wall at this point, sloping it slightly upwards so that any rainwater getting behind the baseplate cannot run through to the interior, and then thread a length of cable through. Leave a generous amount for connection to the light fitting.

Indoors, either cut chases so you can recess the cable into the wall surface (figs. 1 and 2), or else surface-mount it in mini-trunking. Complete the wiring, according to the method you have selected, right back to the point where it will be connected into the existing house wiring, but don't connect it up yet. Wire up the switch—one-gang or

two-gang, according to your system requirements—as shown in figs. F, G and H.

## Fixing the light
With most outside lights, you connect the cable cores directly to a small terminal block on or within the baseplate. The terminals may be marked L, N and E, or you may see short flex tails (colour-coded brown for live, blue for neutral and green/yellow for earth) running to a plastic terminal strip. If there is no earth terminal, check that the fitting is marked as being double-insulated.

With the cable connected up, attach the light baseplate to the wall with screws and wallplugs, and run a bead of clear silicone mastic round the base-

plate/wall junction to keep rainwater from penetrating it.

## Connecting up the power
The final step is to connect up your new sub-circuit to the rest of the house wiring. Start by turning off the power at the main fusebox or consumer unit and then remove the fuse from the circuit concerned (if you have miniature circuit breakers, simply turn off the appropriate mcb). Check that the circuit is indeed dead by plugging in an appliance or turning on a light. Then make your final connections to the rose, socket or circuit cable as required.

If you are at all uncertain about making these final connections (or any part of the job), play safe and call in a qualified electrician.

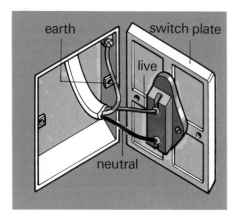

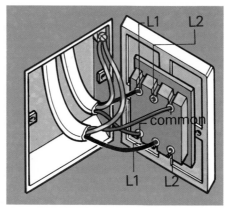

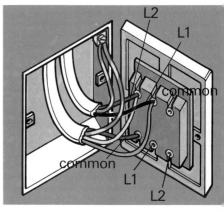

**F**. *If you are using a one-gang switch to control your new light, connect the red and black cores as shown and run the earth core to the box terminal*

**G**. *If you are running the new light's switch cable down to the hall light position, fit a two-gang switch wired up as shown*

**H**. *If you are installing an outside switch too, link it to the indoor switch with three-core and earth cable to provide two-way switching*